ORDINARY PEOPLE
AND
EXTRAORDINARY
EVIL

ORDINARY PEOPLE AND EXTRAORDINARY EVIL

A Report on the Beguilings of Evil

FRED E. KATZ

State University
of New York
Press

Published by
State University of New York Press, Albany

For information, address State University of New York
Press, State University Plaza, Albany, NY 12246

Production by Susan Geraghty
Marketing by Fran Keneston

Library of Congress Cataloging-in-Publication Data

Katz, Fred E..
    Ordinary people and extraordinary evil : a report on the
beguilings of evil / Fred E. Katz.
        p.   cm.
    Includes bibliographical references and index.
    ISBN 0–7914–1441–8 (alk. paper) : $39.50. — ISBN 0–7914–1442–6
(pbk. : alk paper) : $12.95
    1. Good and evil—Case studies. 2. Good and evil—Psychological
aspects. I. Title.
BJ1401.K38   1993
170—dc20
                                                           92–15578
                                                           CIP

10 9 8 7 6 5 4 3

This book is dedicated to the memory of Ludwig, my half-brother. Ludwig's life began in horror. His mother died while giving birth to Ludwig. Twenty-two years later Ludwig's life ended in the Nazi horror. In those twenty-two years Ludwig gave a love to life that is still with me, and nurtures me to this day.

This book faces the future in a spirit of hope. It looks beyond horrors. It does so because of a message derived from Ludwig's life. The message is that horrors are real. But horrors need not defeat us.

"If only there were evil people somewhere, insidiously committing evil deeds, and it were necessary only to separate them from the rest of us and destroy them. But the line dividing good and evil cuts through the heart of every human being. And who is willing to destroy a piece of his own heart?"

—Aleksandr Solzhenitsyn
The Gulag Archipelago

"Monsters exist, but they are too few in number to be truly dangerous. More dangerous are the common man, the functionaries ready to believe and to act without asking questions..."

—Primo Levi
Survival in Auschwitz

CONTENTS

ACKNOWLEDGMENTS

This book was written over a span of ten years. During this time I had the opportunity to try out ideas on students, colleagues, and friends in many places. I shall not even attempt to identify them and thank them individually. Let me say, only, that students at the College of Notre Dame, members of the Department of History at Johns Hopkins University, and fellow congregants at Beth Am synagogue in Baltimore were exceedingly helpful.

During the ten years three of my former teachers died. Of these I mention Frederick Crownfield, and his contributions, in the text of the book. I am also grateful to the other two, William Noland and Harvey Smith, both teachers of mine at the University of North Carolina at Chapel Hill. Bill Noland introduced me to the field of industrial sociology, showing me that work careers and work settings are subjects worth investigating. In some ways this book is about work careers and work settings, derived from Bill Noland's pointers.

Harvey Smith was my major professor, the supervisor of my dissertation and the coordinator of my graduate program. But he was much more than that. Harvey Smith had a singular passion for sociology. For him sociology was a calling and a craft, demanding a total commitment from its adherent and returning to its adherent nothing less than a perspective on life; it was a living faith. For him sociology was also an art, to be practiced creatively and savored for its ways of illuminating our social world. His passion for sociology was on regular display in a unique weekly seminar, which all of his students attended and in which we served our apprenticeship under this exuberant master craftsman.

I cannot point to specific ideas in this book which came from Harvey Smith. But if this book contains any joy in lighting intellectual fires—any joy in formulating ideas and then doggedly and pleasurably seeing where they will lead us—that joy was surely kindled for me by Harvey Smith.

More specific influences on this book were by Maria Coughlin and Stephanie Lebelle, for editorial help in the early stages; Elly Lampner, for carefully reading and commenting on a draft of the manuscript; anonymous readers assigned by SUNY Press, who produced valuable critical comments; and Diane Kempler, for patience beyond the call of duty in word processing. Many thanks to each of you.

I gratefully acknowledge permission from the following sources. From George Weidenfeld and Nicolson Limited (London) and Wydawnictwo Prawnicze (Warsaw) and the Comité International des Camps (Vienna) to cite material from Rudolf Hoess, *Commandant of Auschwitz*. From Odette Komroff to cite material from Fyodor Dostoevski, *The Brothers Karamazov.* From the editors of the journal *Judaism* and Kenneth R. Seeskin to use material from Kenneth Seeskin, "The Reality of Radical Evil," published in *Judaism*. From Panstwowe Muzeum (Oswiecim) to cite material from Jadwiga Bezwinska and Danuta Czech, *KL Auschwitz Seen by the SS*. From the Putnam Publishing Group and Harold Matson Co. to cite material from *The Court-Martial of Lt. Calley* by Richard Hammer, copyright © 1971 by Richard Hammer. From Seymour Hersh to cite from Seymour Hersh, *My Lai 4: A Report on the Massacre and Its Aftermath*. I also wish to say that I am grateful for the use of material from Bernd Naumann, *Auschwitz: A Report on the Proceedings against Robert Karl, Ludwig Mulka and Others Before the Court at Frankfurt* (published by Praeger, in 1966), for which I was unable to identify and locate the current coypright holder.

INTRODUCTION:
FROM THE ORDINARY
TO THE EXTRAORDINARY

This book emerged from an unexpected collision between my profession and my personal story. From that collision I learned that ordinary people, engaging in ordinary behavior, have contributed to extraordinary evil; that every one of us is, on occasion, just a hair's breadth away from contributing mightily to evil; that moral sickness and degeneracy will give us fewer cues about evildoing than will an unemotional look at some quite mundane attributes of our personal and societal makeup—and these attributes can be used for doing evil just as readily as for doing good. What is more, these attributes can be known and understood. We need not remain ignorant and impotent against evil.

The book builds on these ideas. Confronting evil began, for me, in rather private ways of trying to come to terms with having been a victim of evil. It turns out that confronting evil is more than a private matter. Not only are there many persons who become innocent victims of evil. There are also many persons who, beginning innocently, take part in producing and sustaining evil. Their evildoing is encouraged by beguilings of evil—of evil being attractive and rewarding. But there is much ignorance about these beguilings and their role in producing evil. That ignorance need not continue. By conquering it one will become more realistic about how evil is actually produced. Armed with this knowledge we may, from there, turn away from numb and dumb victimization by evil and move toward the life-affirming activity of asserting control over evil. That is an agenda for the future. Meanwhile here, in this book, is a beginning, an in-depth look at the beguilings of evil in action as ordinary people produce extraordinary evil.

1

Evil was not a topic we took seriously during my graduate-student days. Evil seemed to be of concern only to religious fundamentalists and professional philosophers, and not to those of us who were trying to understand people's social behavior scientifically. Hence one of history's major eruptions of evil, the Nazi Holocaust, was not included in our studies. I do not recall hearing the Holocaust mentioned in any of my classes. This pleased me. I did not want to hear about the Holocaust.

I am a Holocaust survivor. My parents and my brother did not survive. Yet from the time I discovered their fate, in 1946, I did no deliberate reading focused on the Holocaust for twenty-seven years. During this time I read none of that litany of Holocaust horrors which nowadays is all-too-familiar to most of us. To be sure I read daily newspapers and I heard newscasts on the radio. I was not out of touch with reality. And in a general sort of way I did know about the Holocaust, including information that came out at the war-crimes trials of some of the perpetrators. But I did not deliberately set out to investigate what had actually happened in the Holocaust.

More important, I made no effort to develop any kind of explanation beyond the then-existing conventional wisdom that here were horrors beyond the realm of understanding, that a singular group of monsters—led by Hitler—had been at work, and that a series of historical circumstances, including a great eruption of anti-Semitism, had culminated in an event that was as unfathomable as it was unique.

I did not consciously set out to remain ignorant about the Holocaust. My approach was largely subconscious. But my actions—of remaining so ignorant and so scientifically inactive—speak rather loudly. Here I was, a professional behavioral scientist who simply remained blind to the major horror of this century, a horror that had decimated my own family and forced me into a most turbulent and rudderless childhood and adolescence.

I awoke to the Holocaust after I accepted a position as a professor of sociology at Tel Aviv University in Israel. There, in Israel, I encountered Holocaust survivors with whom I had much in common—the sort of persons I had strenuously avoided meeting while I lived in the United States. In these survivors I saw myself. I could no longer hide from myself, from my own history, from the real fate of my parents and my brother. It was a harsh encounter, but largely internal to myself. It took its toll on my family and on my ability to establish roots in the land of Israel; I returned to America. And I began to address the Holocaust professionally.

On the professional side, I realized that the Holocaust was a topic that had received far too little attention from my fellow sociologists. To be sure, an enormous amount of Holocaust information was being assembled. It came from historians, political scientists, psychologists, and most of all, from lay-persons and humanists. Information on what actually happened was being amassed in unprecedented quantity. And there were beginning to be memorials and commemorations, on a large scale.

Despite a virtual deluge of information about the Holocaust, it struck me that the distinctive imagination of behavioral scientists was not yet being tapped.[1] Perhaps most of us were so focused on the horror of the horrors that we could not be dispassionate in our thinking, thereby preventing ourselves from developing explanations that go beyond the conventional wisdom. Like most persons who reflected about the Holocaust, we dwelled on its utter uniqueness.

For some persons the sense of the Holocaust's uniqueness included the expectation that if the full extent of the horrors were known—if people saw the depth of depravity that took place—then people will be so appalled that such horrors will not be repeated; that knowledge of the horrors will serve as a vaccine against future horrors. I was always uncomfortable with this belief. Are there not persons who are actually attracted to horrors, and want to repeat them?

It gradually dawned on me that horrors can yield insights which can free us from the impotence we still have in the face of outbreaks of great evil. But to accomplish this it is not enough to remember what happened when evil prevailed. It is not enough, even, to sanctify the memory and fate of loved ones who became victims. We do have a duty to remember what happened when evil prevailed. Yet the greatest challenge is to develop *effective* knowledge, and this goes far beyond remembering and documenting what happened. We must go beyond dwelling on the horror of the horrors.

Here my background as scientist reasserted itself. I remained convinced that the history of science teaches us that to understand unusually horrible events one needs to understand *ordinary* events. That one crucial ingredient in the scientist's posture—the scientist's way of looking at the world—is to look for the ordinary in order to explain the extraordinary. I believe this applies to understanding and combating extraordinary evil.

Another ingredient in the scientist's posture is that facts do *not* speak for themselves; facts must be spoken to. This applies even to events as ghastly as those that took place in the Holocaust, events whose character seems so self-evident, apparently speaking for itself with such a clear voice. When we operate as investigators of horrendous events we have to *create* ways of looking at them. And this may lead to looking at these events in ways that are neither obvious nor popular.

The seeds for the insight that scientists must create ways of looking were sown in me by Frederick Crownfield, a teacher of mine at Guilford College, where I received my undergraduate schooling. Fred Crownfield had doctoral-level training in physics, religion, and philosophy. He left me with an incurable addiction to the work and thinking of Alfred North Whitehead, one of his teachers at Harvard University and a giant in the fields of philosophy and mathematics. If I see *creativity* as a necessary part of the scientific process I am, of course, following Whitehead. I affectionately blame Fred Crownfield, he guided me onto this track. After these words were written, and before I had a chance to show them to him, Fred Crownfield, this inspiring teacher, died.

Translated into practice, the two ingredients of the scientist's posture mean that we must seek the clues to the causes of horrendously evil behavior, such as the mass murders and dehumanization that took place in the Holocaust, in ordinary everyday behavior of ordinary people.

It means that we may need to go through the wrenching experience of rejecting what seems so clearly self-evident as "causing" evil. This includes rejecting the notion that only fanatics and sick people do evil (we tell ourselves that emotionally healthy people do not do evil); that leaders are primarily responsible for evil (as though leaders did not need a host of followers to implement their programs); and, finally, that only evil people do evil (of course the statement that evil people do evil explains very little, and it assumes that evildoers are very different from the rest of us).

It means we have to, intellectually, raise ourselves by our own bootstraps; we have to create new ways of looking while we are looking at ordinary behavior. Within the scientific process, having to create ways of looking has sometimes led to sublime discoveries from looking at seemingly ordinary events, such as deriving the law of gravitation from observing the fall of an apple from a tree (be it apocryphal or not, this has long served as a bellwether in teaching students how to think scientifically). Powerful knowledge is to be derived from paying attention to the ordinary, provided we do it creatively.

EVIL DEFINED

I define and use the word *evil* to mean behavior that deliberately deprives innocent people of their humanity, from small scale assaults on a person's dignity to outright murder. This is a *behavioral* definition of evil. It focuses on how people behave toward one another—where the behavior of one person, or an aggregate of persons, is destructive to others.

Evil is commonly seen in religious, moral and philosophical terms: as violating higher commandments, as breaking valued constraints that bind us to other persons, or as making us depart from a benign deity in favor of following a malignant deity, a satan. I do not deny that these are important, even profound ways of considering evil. I shall not delve into them because it would distract from what I want to accomplish here; namely showing that a behavioral view of evil helps us confront it. We thereby lift evil out of the realm of the supernatural and place it squarely in the realm of day-to-day living.

When I say that a behavioral approach to evil will help us confront evil, I do not mean to say that we will henceforth avoid evil, that evil will no longer happen. I mean, only, that it will enable us to know more realistically how evil is produced. And from this more realistic knowledge we will be in a better position to avoid traveling the road to evil, if we so choose. We shall see road signs where we previously did not see road signs.

LOOKING AT EVIL BEHAVIORALLY

I am not the first to try to see evil, particularly the extreme evil of the Holocaust, in terms of the behavior of individuals. Among psychologists of the 1940s and 1950s there was an upsurge of research to understand the causes of such behavior. Of these Theodore Adorno and his colleagues claimed that when individuals had an *authoritarian personality* they tended to unquestioningly obey instructions, whatever these instructions might be.[2] Later Stanley Milgram, another American psychologist, examined *obedience to authority* in a series of laboratory experiments that focused on how people would actually behave when under pressure to inflict injury on innocent persons. Milgram believed that obedience to authority was the crucial ingredient in the individual's willingness to take part in what I am calling evil behavior. His experiments were repeated in Munich, Rome, South Africa, and Australia, with roughly comparable results.[3]

I shall suggest a modification of Milgram's obedience to authority theme. One can be caught in a process of beguilement by evil, of seduction into doing evil by the immediate circumstances in which one finds oneself. This can happen when we find ourselves in a social setting where the immediate circumstances dominate our entire field of moral vision. Here the larger society's values and even our own upbringing that taught us to treat people humanely can be disregarded and new, locally generated values take their place.[4] "Obedience to authority" may not be an issue at all; one may do evil to please one's peers, or for one of many other reasons—even for personal enjoyment. Here the one feature that dominates all others is that the immediate context in which one finds oneself shuts out the outside world's values, leaving one vulnerable to new "values."

I shall have us take a look at this and four additional forms of beguilement into doing evil. The four additional forms are:

- the packaging of evil: making evil an acceptable commodity to individuals who are not necessarily predisposed to doing evil;

- careerism and its potential for creating a person's route to evil: much of it through small, incremental, and innocent decisions;

- bureaucratization of evil: moral bankruptcy amid orderliness, when bureaucratic procedures are harnessed for producing evil;

- creation of a separate and distinct culture of cruelty: where evildoing becomes enjoyable and rewarding to a group of people.

A precursor to this book's line of thinking about evil is Hannah Arendt's theme of the banality of evil.[5] Arendt developed it in her description of Adolf Eichmann during his trial for murderous crimes. Eichmann was a major contributor to the entire extermination program of the Nazis. Arendt pointed to Eichmann's ordinariness—in the way he conducted his career, in the way he saw the world—when all around her at the trial of Eichmann there was a clamor for depicting him as the very embodiment of evil. Arendt left us with the crucial insight that evil, even evil on a horrendous scale, can be practiced by very ordinary sorts of persons. But she did not spell out for us how human ordinariness can be so readily harnessed for evil. I shall try to answer that challenge by addressing two tasks.

First, I try to clarify *impediments* to accepting, and acting upon, the insight that ordinary people, using ordinary behavior, can produce extraordinary evil. I point out that dwelling on the uniqueness of the Holocaust is such an impediment and so is the notion that the Holocaust, and other large scale horrors, are incomprehensible; that horrors of this scale are simply beyond our capacity to explain. Both of these views are held by very earnest people, many of whom were personally traumatized by the Holocaust. Although I take issue with these views, I do so with a spirit of great respect for those holding them. I believe that a sense of the uniqueness of the Holocaust can be preserved while, at the same time, placing it in the confines of human behavior that can be explained.

Second, I suggest some *attributes of ordinary human behavior* that are conducive to producing evil, be they carried out by participants in evil or not. The attributes are first described in a rather theoretical way, then their applicability is shown in case studies of four individuals: an American physician, whom I am calling Dr. Doe (not his real name), who is an exemplary human being and not a participant in evil at all; Rudolf Hoess, who was in charge of the Auschwitz extermination camp; Dr. Johann Paul Kremer, an SS physician, who, too, was at Auschwitz; and Lieutenant William Calley and the My Lai events in Vietnam, where the zeal of soldiers in battle, though deviating from our humane values, is a long way removed, morally and practically, from the horrors of Auschwitz. Let me repeat, the American physician is not engaged in evil at all. And Lieutenant Calley's actions at My Lai are not in the same evil league as the actions of the perpetrators of Auschwitz.

I refer to My Lai and the events of Vietnam with a heavy heart because, as I write these words, young American men and women were once again called to serve as soldiers in a distant land. Many of their parents served in the jungles of Vietnam. They, in turn, were called to serve in the deserts of the Middle East. Once again these Americans, our sons and daughters, were asked to fight in a land whose language they did not speak, whose customs they did not know, whose values they only vaguely comprehended, and whose climate is extreme. And thanks to the marvels of modern technology, they were transported to this setting very quickly, without much time to learn what the fight was all about.

These young American soldiers acquitted themselves with great honor. They gave to America their full measure of courage and devotion, up to donating their very lives, just as their fathers and grandfathers had done when they were called upon to fight in wars. And yet. And yet. The Vietnam veterans still suffering from Posttraumatic Stress disease are telling us very eloquently about the price of horrors in battles. Among them the outbreak of war in the Persian Gulf produced a large-scale reactivation of their nightmares. They are teaching us, through their illness, through their suffering at this moment, that soldiers, like all human beings, are *moral* creatures, whose participation in horrors does not happen lightly. We owe it to them to take a very frank look at the horrors in which entirely decent human beings can become active participants. For this reason the events of My Lai are still relevant.

I include Lieutenant Calley and My Lai, specifically, for three reasons. One, to show that evil comes in varying degrees; we have the unmatched level of evil in the Nazi Holocaust programs, such as the one at Auschwitz, and we have a far lesser level of evil at My Lai. Two, to illustrate that some of the same forms of ordinary behavior are active in both. Three, to point out that the My Lai participants are as human as the rest of us: they are not monsters, and neither are we; they are our kin, whom we sent off to war and who remained our kin upon their return; their actions teach us a great deal about how we, humans, adapt to the immediate circumstances in which we find ourselves; and this, in turn, deepens our knowledge of our own humanity in the face of the real world in which we exist.

A major lesson the My Lai events teach us is that the setting in which one finds oneself can be a powerful generator of new behavior. This behavior may deviate greatly from wider societal values. And it can become very seductive. This can happen when the setting is sufficiently separated from its surroundings. The immediate local circumstances can then dominate one's moral vision and one's behavior.

We confront a real challenge when we have to explain that people very much like ourselves can be willing and eager participants in evil; that we can be beguiled by evil. I believe that we can know how these processes work, and once we do so, we are in a better position to avoid doing evil, provided we want to do so. But there are obstacle to be overcome. One of these is the belief that only human monsters are responsible for evil.

Ours is a culture of optimism—of hope and opportunity for bettering oneself, of belief in human dignity, of the real possibility of living a life that contributes something of value to ourselves and to the world in which we live. Much of what we see and experience still confirms and reinforces this view. Yet alongside it ours is a world that contains a litany of misery, of really enormous evil. And what is more, we seem to be quite helpless in the face of such evil. We are often caught by surprise when major evil erupts. And we are frequently too late to keep it from reaching horrendous levels.

Do we need not remain so helpless in the face of evil? Can we attain more effective knowledge of how massive evil can happen, and from this, improve the ability to prevent it? To do so we need to adopt a new way of thinking about evil, a way that looks for the foundation of evil, not in human monsters—the Hitlers and Stalins of the world—but in ordinary human behavior that all of us share. I shall adopt this way of thinking about evil in order to use it as a vehicle to take us on a journey of learning into the lives of some individuals, evildoers as well as genuinely good persons.

IS EVIL REAL?

Yes

In this century alone well over a hundred million persons have met a violent death at the hands of their fellow human beings. This includes the military killings in the two World Wars, the deliberate annihilation of Jews by Nazis and Armenians by Turks, the bloodbaths during and after the Russian and Chinese Revolutions (the two revolutions are conservatively estimated to have produced 35 million deaths), and the killings in Cambodia and Biafra. It also includes deliberate mass starvation, most notably Stalin's program that starved to death some 14 million peasants in the early 1930s. This list is not complete, but it is surely long enough. Let us bear in mind that it does not include those who were maimed and continued their lives just short of death. Their number, too, runs into the millions.

If we accept my definition of evil, that it is behavior ranging from deliberate destruction of human dignity to deliberate destruction of human life, then evil is indeed real. And if extraordinary evil is defined as this kind of behavior on a huge scale, then this century has amassed a record of extraordinary evil.

There are two striking aspects to such evil. It is largely the handiwork of ordinary sorts of people; it is banal, as Hannah Arendt taught us. And, despite this, it is still very poorly understood. As a result we remain largely impotent in the face of extraordinary evil. Yet, I repeat, I believe we can reduce our impotence by improving our understanding of the processes that create evil.

WHO PRODUCES EXTRAORDINARY EVIL?

Ordinary People, Like You and Me

Only a tiny proportion of this century's massive killings are attributable to the actions of those people we call criminals, or crazy people, or socially alienated people, or even, people we identify as evil people. The vast majority of killings were actually carried out by plain folk in the population—ordinary people, like you and me. Hence, in respect to mass killings, we must worry every bit as much about the actions of ordinary human beings as about the actions of crackpots and criminals.

What about the leaders? Does not the responsibility for evil rest with leaders who manipulate their people to do their bidding? Were not the Germans under the influence of Hitler? Were not the Soviets up to the early 1950s, under the influence of Stalin? Do not leaders cause their followers to do things that these followers do not really want to do?

Certainly the Hitlers and Stalins of our world produced plans for evil that boggle the mind. But who transformed these plans into action? Ordinary people, like you and me. To begin with, who provides the fervor and zeal? Ordinary people, like you and me. Using Germany as an example, there people roared themselves hoarse and reached states of high ecstasy as they responded to Hitler's speeches. To Hitler and his cause they donated their energies, their skill, and their very lives, often doing so with joyful abandon.

Who provides the intelligence, the brain power, the orderly thinking to translate crazy philosophies into a practical course of action? Ordinary people, like you and me. For Hitler, a multitude of administrative bureaucrats and highly educated professionals—engineers, architects, economists, physicians and lawyers—worked to transform his vision of a racially pure Germany into a reality, donating their expertise and professional skills. And among Germany's military officers the vast majority were only too willing to translate Hitler's dream of military glory into a practical course of action.

Who provides the quiet sustained effort, the plain hard work it takes to carry out huge programs of murderous action? Ordinary people, like you and me. The willing servants of Hitler, his foot soldiers, were ordinary Germans, not a specially selected cadre of fanatics.

How can one understand and, perhaps, forestall extraordinary evil? *By getting better understanding of how ordinary behavior can contribute to evil.*

To understand how extraordinary evil is planned, organized and carried out we need to look beyond the dreams and actions of human monsters, the Hitlers of the world. We need to look at *ordinary* behavior to understand *extraordinary* evil. The task is not easy. First we must overcome more of our traditional thinking about evil (in addition to the belief that only monsters produce evil, already mentioned).

We live in a world that is periodically polluted by eruptions of humanly created evil, often resulting in deliberately created deaths on a huge scale, in one or another part of the globe. On a smaller scale, but still involving a lot of people, we have the very high crime rates in American cities, where human life is deemed cheap and expendable. And, in America of the 1980s, we saw the age of greed, where the federal government condoned and encouraged focus on one's own self-interest, and the poor were left to suffer indignity upon indignity.

Our response to the eruption of deaths on a huge scale is to regard each eruption as a local event, carried out by a set of unique evildoers. We tell ourselves that these actions, although abhorrent, are deviations from the routines of daily living. Hence, we say, if we can find the top leaders, and punish them, we can cleanse societies from evil and return to the routines of daily living. Yet this flies in the face of the fact that this "cleansing" seems to produce no immunity against the next round of horrors. Either there are plenty more "deviant" individuals, waiting to lead a course of evil when an opportunity arises, or far more likely, the search for individual evildoers is the wrong approach.

To the high crime rate in our cities we respond by distancing ourselves. Those able to do so have long ago moved out of the city; or if living within the city, they insulate themselves from the fearsome realities of life in the depressed neighborhoods. Life in the neighborhoods where daily drug-related killings take place is not regarded as normal, as being within the range of the ordinary but needing to be addressed, except in terms of police protection of the more affluent neighborhoods.

In the generation of greed we responded by giving public glorification to those who gained great wealth. We gave them our envy and our adulation. We did not ask searching questions about their route to riches.

The generation of greed was built on an ethic that said our social order is based on self-interest, the individual comes first. Here, too, there was a process of distancing, of assuming that evil was not real. The ethic claimed that the needs of the disadvantaged are of no serious concern to the unaffected citizen, to employers, and even to the government. The result of this was not evil in the form of large scale outright murder, but large scale assault on human dignity—in the form of high rates of poverty, untended disease among the disadvantaged, loss of occupational careers and neglect of public services. It was assumed, under the self-interest ethic, that this was the natural order of things, that one need not attack it as a moral issue to which the larger community should respond. Yet it takes a very short political memory to see that this ethic has not always reigned supreme in America, nor does it reign supreme in most other so-called advanced countries.

The human indignities of the 1980s were a human creation, requiring a great deal of human effort to bring them about. Yet they were not created by people who had horns on their head, who deliberately set out to do evil. Many of the indignities were created by people pursuing personal careers, who did not deliberately and intentionally set out to hurt other people. They were bent on accumulating as much money and property for themselves as they could. Their contribution to evil was not at all obvious to themselves. I will show later on that even the most flagrant evil, as in some of the Holocaust actions, can be performed by persons who do not recognize that what they are doing is evil or, more commonly, that evil can be done by persons who act on the basis of priorities that are not obviously evil.

The route to evil often takes the form of a sequence of seemingly small, innocuous incremental steps, in each of which one tries to solve a problem within one's immediate situation. This approach to living, so customary in the daily life of most of us, can lead to ignoring other people's well-being. In the 1980s the stockmarket insider trading scandals, coupled with "creative financing" for buccaneering takeovers, served as examples of persons using a series of seemingly small innocuous incremental steps to participate in evil. These persons pursued advantageous "deals" with vigor and ingenuity, tempted by how small transgressions of the rules could offer enormous financial rewards. Once engaged in this practice the financial rewards were so vast, and the means to achieve it so readily available within their immediate world (that is, they could rob without having to openly hold up banks), that some of the brightest persons fed on an orgy of greed that destroyed many a company and the livelihood of many an innocent person. In this whirl of self-aggrandizement the wider society's morality came to be regarded as quite irrelevant. For some executives their own immediate route to prosperity was all that counted. While following this route they treated their employees as throwaway property, while they themselves obtained huge financial gains.

Further on I shall illustrate a comparable personal career route—made up, also, of a sequence of seemingly small innocuous incremental steps—but leading to far cruder evil. I shall do so by examining in detail the history and career of Rudolf Hoess, the man in charge of the Auschwitz concentration camp.

The larger point is that such ordinary human behavior—as concentrating on one's career and adhering to the rules of a bureaucracy in which one works—can just as easily be used to participate in evil as in humane activities. But there are real gaps in our understanding of how this works. This book will try to fill some of these gaps. When we understand some ordinary behavior better we will be less surprised by evil, we will be less likely to be unwitting contributors to evil, we will be able to tell when we approach the threshold between good and evil, and we will be better equipped to forestall evil.

OVERVIEW OF THE BOOK

The main question this book considers is, Precisely how can ordinary behavior contribute to evil?

In much of what follows the Holocaust is used to illustrate extraordinary evil. The Holocaust serves as a metaphor for evil—as an example of extraordinary evil in action, as an aid in explaining responses to evil, and as a reservoir of information about the ways in which evil is produced—to help us confront evil dispassionately. To be sure the Holocaust contains unique elements, as does every instance of extraordinary evil, but it also contains elements that are generalizable, and therefore applicable to understanding other instances of extraordinary evil.

The first two chapters develop some concepts for explaining how ordinary behavior can go so terrible awry. These concepts may be applied to common occurrences, such as personal illness and how people make choices that affect their careers. But the chief reason for paying attention to them here, in this book, is because they can apply to ordinary people's participation in extraordinary evil.

The bulk of this book consists of case studies. These include a close look at three contributors to evil: the head of the Auschwitz camp; a physician who also worked at Auschwitz; and, at a far lesser level of evil, an American officer in Vietnam. But first, as comparative background, there will be a brief glimpse of the professional life of an exemplary physician who typifies some of the ordinary behaviors that could be used—but were not used—in the service of evil. The largest case study is that of the head of the Auschwitz camp. His story demonstrates many dimensions of a life of evil built upon foundations of ordinary behavior.[6]

The first three chapters concentrate on how evil is produced. The last chapter includes a glimpse of the larger picture and suggests ways of turning away from evil. It offers some practical tips on how to counteract the beguilings of evil by using what was learned in the previous portions. Its guiding thesis is that just as the production of evil requires use of our ordinary behavior, so does turning away from evil. The same patterns of ordinary behavior give us weapons for counteracting evil and freeing us from contributing to evil. We may still choose to be doers of evil. But we need not remain unwitting doers of evil.

CHAPTER 1

Confronting Evil and Its Paradoxes

He was "a very ordinary little man." So said an amazed Bertrand Russell, one of the great philosophers of this century, in describing a man who sat in court shortly after the Second World War facing charges of committing horrendous crimes. Indeed, the man was not an impressive figure. If anything he was average looking, perhaps a bit overweight. His manner was mild. He had none of the master-race arrogance commonly associated with the Nazi ideologist. In Russell's view, he gave no sign of great brilliance, cunning or malevolence. In the course of the court hearings the man was very forthcoming in his answers to questions, seemingly not hiding anything. He appeared eager to bring out all the facts.

The accused man was Rudolf Hoess, the chief of the Auschwitz concentration camp. Hoess had been in charge of setting up the camp, and he had been the major architect for planning its program. He had devised many of its specific methods of torture and murder. He remained in overall charge of the camp during most of its period of existence. He was its ongoing supervisor and enforcer of operations.

Hoess, who looked so ordinary, was perhaps the greatest executioner of human beings of all times. Over 2 million persons were put to death under his orders. The victims included the whole range of humankind. There were the young and old, the healthy and sick, the married and single, the religious and irreligious, the educated and uneducated. Hoess was the main functionary who saw to it that their voices were stilled forever. How could a seemingly ordinary man make such a contribution to extraordinary evil?

In contrast to Hoess, Bertrand Russell was not an ordinary man—he was one of this century's intellectual giants. He made profound contributions to philosophy, and his innovations in mathematics underlie much of the computer revolution we are now experiencing. But beyond that, he was one of the leading voices that advocated a modern Age of Reason.

Russell was fond of saying that the greatest mission of all was "extending the sphere of reason" to new realms of living.[1] He believed that reason, humankind's marvelous capacity for understanding the world around us, could be used to tackle many problems that cause human misery. It could improve our lives if we but allow it to operate in areas where we traditionally rely upon superstition and fuzzy thinking. And the process of reasoning, itself, could be continually sharpened and used to help us understand more of the puzzles in the world around us.

Yet here, in the person of Hoess, was a puzzle that resisted reason: How could a seemingly limited little man make such a prodigious contribution to evil?

Hoess embodied a paradox: *When it comes to doing evil deeds, a very ordinary person may make very extraordinary contributions.*

And furthermore, the life of Hoess shows, as we shall see later on in Chapter 3 when Hoess's life is examined more fully, that an ordinary person may not only do evil, but do evil innovatively and enthusiastically and on a grand scale. The book will explore the Hoess paradox by dwelling on the question, how does ordinary behavior contribute to extraordinary evil?

ARENDT'S VIEW OF EICHMANN

Hannah Arendt also pointed to the ordinariness of those who carried out the mass murders of the Nazi era. Her book on Adolf Eichmann's trial is subtitled *A Report on the Banality of Evil.*[2]

Eichmann had been in charge of organizing the transportation of Jews to the concentration and extermination camps. In this capacity he was responsible for arranging that a steady flow of victims would be delivered to the camps. He thereby had a major role in the bureaucratic administration of the extermination program; and he played this role with unyielding persistence, considerable ingenuity, and great verve. About fifteen years after the Second World War Israeli agents captured Eichmann in his hiding place in Argentina and brought him to trial in Israel. Hannah Arendt's book describes the trial.

In Arendt's view the Eichmann trial was a partial failure. Certainly it was a considerable accomplishment to bring to trial a person who was a central participant in the unprecedented mass murders, a person who contributed so greatly to the annihilation of so many innocent persons. The prosecution believed that now they might be able to use Eichmann to personify the horror, the evil, that had been perpetrated. But Eichmann turned out to be a very ordinary sort of bureaucrat. He might have been exceedingly and bizarrely confused about ideological and moral issues, but he had a strong sense of dignity, orderliness, commitment to what he saw as a grand cause. His conscience was warped—"he would have had a bad conscience only if he had not done what he had been ordered to do—to ship millions of men, women and children to their death with great zeal and meticulous care"[3]—but *he seemingly did have a conscience.*

This was hard to accept. Arendt wrote: "Half a dozen psychiatrists certified him as a 'normal'—'more normal, at any rate, than I am after having examined him' one of them was said to have exclaimed."[4]

The prosecution made desperate efforts to bring out the man's viciousness, the pure evil that they felt must surely reside in him. They did succeed in documenting the horrors committed by the Nazis. They went to excruciating lengths to enumerate the deeds that took place, and Eichmann certainly had a great part in these deeds. But *he,* as an individual, emerges as an incredibly ordinary, banal person. His mental horizon was not very large, but he did not appear to be a person who was driven by evil motives as such. He was a person strongly committed to getting his personal fulfillment through a bureaucratic career. He took his work awfully seriously. He took the Nazi cause, with its anti-Semitic ideology, awfully seriously.

In short, Eichmann came through his trial looking like a thoroughly ordinary bureaucrat. He was not mentally ill, as the psychiatrists had to admit. Arendt wrote: "The trouble with Eichmann was precisely that so many were like him, and that the many were neither perverted, nor sadistic, that they were, and still are, terribly and terrifyingly normal."[5]

The prosecutors at the trial, the survivors of Eichmann's efforts, and very many other people, Jews and non-Jews alike, found this very hard to accept. After all, the deeds in which Eichmann participated so enthusiastically and energetically speak for themselves. They are ghoulish in the extreme—in their scope, in their bestiality—and they defy comparison with most other inhumanities.

The trial ended with the death sentence for Eichmann. (This was not surprising, not even to Eichmann himself. During the trial he occasionally remarked, "Don't you have enough to hang me already?") The prosecution, given its herculean efforts to document the horrendous crimes, appeared satisfied. It remained for Arendt, in her role as an observer for *The New Yorker* magazine, to give public expression to the *banality* of Eichmann, to define his terrible ordinariness. This proved to be a very upsetting idea. It produced widespread shock and anger.[6]

The victims of Nazism felt there was nothing "ordinary" about their experiences. They believed the catalogue of Nazi horrors showed a program of genocide that was surely unique in the history of humankind; and they held that Eichmann, as a major organizer of the Nazi program, in all its horrendous ramifications, was surely not behaving as an ordinary person. How could one regard such deeds, and such a man, as banal or ordinary?

Of course these people were right. There was nothing ordinary in the scale and ferocity of the Nazi program of extermination of innocent human beings. It is an obscenity to trivialize it, as some have done, by equating it with other crimes, and various lesser social injustices. The Nazi Holocaust was evil at its most extreme, and Eichmann was an active, innovative and exuberant participant in that evil.

However, the voices of this very justified passion can lead one astray. Surviving victims and their kin are inflamed by the memory of those innocents whose lives were extinguished, those brothers and sisters, those fathers and mothers, those children. Eichmann's *deeds* were monstrous, but Eichmann was also thoroughly ordinary. If we are not prepared to accept this fact, and to learn from it, then we are losing an opportunity to understand evil and, perhaps, to prevent it in future.[7]

The actions of Eichmann, for which he was tried and convicted, were extraordinary. There was nothing ordinary about the Nazi Holocaust as carried out by Eichmann and his cohorts. Yet, if we insist on concentrating on the extraordinary side of Eichmann, on the monstrosity of his deeds, we shall remain impotent against evil. If we merely put a "monster" label on the man and his deeds, without understanding the very ordinary mechanisms of behavior he utilized, then we cannot understand how the monstrous actions could have taken place. We may continue to be outraged at the Eichmanns of this world, but we shall not forestall future extraordinary evils as long as our level of understanding remains inadequate. We shall remain intellectually crippled by our rage.

To confront evil we must put passion aside, concentrating instead on the real issue: How is the ordinary transformed into the extraordinary? In the case of Eichmann, how did he transform the ordinary into the extraordinary? How much of the ordinary was retained amid Eichmann's world of extraordinary evil? In short, how could a man who was so profoundly ordinary accomplish deeds that were so extraordinary? I shall take up these issues via the case study of Rudolf Hoess, in Chapter 3. Hoess was in a way doing even greater evil than Eichmann. He, like Eichmann, made abundant use of ordinary behavior.

If we understand the ordinary more fully, and if we understand how the ordinary is transformed into the extraordinary, we shall stand a chance of understanding how it is that evil appears and prospers so often.

IS DISPASSIONATE STUDY OF EVIL POSSIBLE?

The public responses to Hannah Arendt's book on Eichmann were very spirited, some quite negative. These responses imply a second paradox: *Those persons most affected by horrendous deeds may unwittingly stand in the way of understanding the causes of the deeds.* The victims, in their passionate—and justified!—espousal of the uniqueness of the horrors that have befallen them, may hinder dispassionate analysis.

Hannah Arendt epitomized the cool, detached observer. Her emphasis was on an unemotional search for facts and dispassionate explanations, especially through comparison of the Holocaust with other forms of authoritarianism. At the heart of this approach is a search for generalizations, for concepts that show how a particular event is comparable to other events. The "uniqueness" of a particular event is regarded as more apparent than real. In Arendt's work on Eichmann she applied detachment to events that Holocaust survivors cannot help seeing in highly personal and utterly unique terms.

This approach applies the scientist's objectivity to the horrendous evil exemplified by the Holocaust. It operates from these assumptions:

- The large-scale brutalization and murder of innocent people in the Holocaust is a manifestation of colossal evil.
- There are many forms of colossal social evil.
- Each is terribly real.
- Each is entirely unique to its victims and their kin
- The Holocaust's importance is not diminished by comparing it to other forms of evil. Indeed, only by making such comparisons, and developing generalizations, can one develop the kind of knowledge that might enable one to prevent future Holocausts.

In contrast to this approach, survivors and descendants of victims of the Nazi Holocaust, like the descendants of the victims of the Turkish massacres of Armenians earlier in the century, to this day, have a living and active sense of immersion in these events. To them, the events are drenched in such personal horror that to them "detachment" amounts to absurdity, if not outright desecration of the memory of those who died. Arendt's scholarly, scientific detachment, with its notion that the Holocaust was a by-product of authoritarian systems that are not at all unique and that its individual perpetrators were ordinary persons, is appalling to many survivors of the Holocaust. They see scientific objectivity as a violation of the full uniqueness of the events that took place.

Survivors have emphasized that the Holocaust has no parallels, that it is incomparable. In practice, this meant that many survivors spent the first years after the Second World War in stunned silence. So great was the catastrophe, so overpowering was its effect, so profound the evil, that for many survivors the only possible response with personal meaning was silence. Silence alone appeared to even approach doing justice to the enormity of the unspeakable events that had taken place. Elie Wiesel, the winner of the 1986 Nobel Peace Prize was, and remains, the most eloquent spokesperson for this view of the enormity and of the fundamental incomprehensibility of the Holocaust. As a survivor of extermination camps and also as an artist and writer, Wiesel spent the first post-Holocaust years in silence. Since then he has increasingly spoken about what he regards as the unspeakable. He senses a compulsion to comprehend Holocaust experiences, but believes that these experiences can never be comprehended. From this viewpoint speaking about the Holocaust is, at best, a step in the direction of comprehension, where full comprehension is inherently impossible.

Following the years of stunned silence, some very different responses to the Holocaust emerged. These included efforts to reconcile the Holocaust with religious teachings. Where was God during the Nazi era? How could God permit such total disaster? Was God absent? Was God incapable of keeping humans from being so inhuman? And, more affirmatively, was God perhaps speaking to Jews and humankind *through* Auschwitz? Is there a religious message that comes from Auschwitz?[8]

In the 1960s a virtual turnabout in responses to the Holocaust began. No longer was silence valued so highly. Instead, there started much deliberate public speaking and writing about the Holocaust. The thinking was that the world must not be allowed to forget what happened. Information about the Holocaust not only must be stored in archives and libraries, it must be publicized. It must be taught in schools. It must be included in everyday discourse about politics, about community life, and about personal life. For many, drawing attention to the Holocaust has become a sacred duty.

Scholars operating in the Hannah Arendt tradition bring yet another interpretation to the Holocaust. They decry the "mystic vision of the Holocaust" that rejects comparing the Holocaust to other forms of mass murder and torture and that denies social scientists the opportunity to develop theories that encompass all kinds of genocide, not merely the Nazi variant. Irving Louis Horowitz (a sociologist, and holder of the Hannah Arendt Professorship at Rutgers University) says: "genocide must be reduced from mass culture...[and] be made part and parcel of a general theory of social systems and social structures, and if social science is to make its own serious contribution to the Holocaust studies it must move beyond the mystery of silence or the silence of mysteries."[9]

It is harsh to say that those who were most directly involved in the Holocaust—its survivors and their kinsfolk—may actually stand in the way of attaining dispassionate and objective knowledge about it. But there is, indeed, a difference between the attitude of victims, trying to come to terms with the evil that has befallen them and the attitude of scientists, trying to discover concepts that explain the occurrence of evil in different times and places. Yet the two can be reconciled when we realize that each is valid, that each serves a distinctive and important purpose, and that neither negates the other.

When one concentrates on the uniqueness of a calamity, such as one's particular encounter with the Holocaust, one is trying to come to terms with the collapse of a significant portion of one's world. One's resulting grief contains a measure of highly personal reality that cannot possibly be generalized. From the survivors' standpoint, trying to generalize from the Holocaust amounts to interfering with one's personal mourning, the sanctity of one's personal memories, and one's personal outrage against the perpetrators. All of these are ways of mentally constructing a meaningful and livable reality for oneself in response to evil events that were, and still are, experienced personally. All of these are addressed by focus on the uniqueness of the evil events.

By contrast, scientists live with different mental constructions. One focuses on objective knowledge and the ability to generalize, rather than giving primacy to personal experience. To accomplish this, a full "experience" of a catastrophe is not necessary. To do research on cancer in the hope of discovering a cure for cancer, the scientist does not have to capture the full experience of the horror of having cancer. One does not deny the personal side of every catastrophe, but one chooses to concentrate on its features that appear in a variety of contexts. To accomplish this one does not attempt to capture the fullness and the essence of the catastrophe as a victim might experience it. Instead, one concentrates on those features that are knowable in an objective way. One's goal is to understand *some features* very well. One looks for generalizations, for laws of behavior that apply to the occurrence of these features in many situations. One's objective is to gain knowledge that will apply to future events and, thereby, prevent future catastrophies.

In actuality, the unique and the generalizing approaches have much in common. Those who emphasize the uniqueness of each instance of horrendous evil also want to prevent similar events in the future. Those who scientifically compare the Holocaust to, say, other forms of authoritarian control also want to honor the memory of the victims of the Holocaust, and they do not deny the unique fate and needs of its surviving victims. But in their central objectives, they differ. And in their methods, they differ.

Now, to begin to look at those who commit horrors, here is another paradox: *Horrendous deeds may be performed by persons who are addressing themselves to innocuous immediate problems.* A person may do horrible things without paying attention to the horror of the deeds, instead focusing attention only on an aspect of the situation that is relatively benign.

A good illustration of this point is contained in Stanley Milgram's experiments I mentioned earlier.[10] For his experiments Milgram set up a laboratory situation in which the subjects thought they were teachers in a learning experiment. If a "learner" made a mistake, the subject (the "teacher") was to administer an electric shock to the learner. When the learner continued to make mistakes the subject was told to increase the severity of the shocks. Eventually the shocks would reach a high level of severity, involving much pain for the learner. In reality the shocks were simulated—there were no electric shocks at all—but the subjects did not know this. The striking finding of the experiments was that most of the subjects were willing to inflict severe pain on the "learners."

Milgram's instructions for the participants mapped out an *immediate context.* It contained two features: the claim that the participant was making an important contribution to science; and the claim that it was necessary to have unquestioning obedience to the instructions. These two features were presented as a complete set of prescriptions governing participation in that context. It left no room for other considerations, such as being worried about inflicting pain on innocent people. Milgram's work showed that the immediate context proved to be a remarkably effective device for getting people to do horrible things. The research participants paid attention chiefly to the instructions they received in that immediate context. The other features—the fact that they were inflicting pain on innocent people—were brushed aside by the administrator of the experiments, and most participants accepted this and did not withdraw from the experiment.

How can one explain such behavior? Why were the subjects willing to inflict pain? Milgram's own interpretation of his findings was that obedience to authority was the crucial factor in making people inflict pain on innocent people (plus their belief that they were making a contribution to science).

I believe that a more realistic interpretation is that people can be mentally locked into a particular context (as Milgram's subjects were; as American soldiers in Vietnam sometimes were; as SS guards in concentration camps often were), where "outside" values are excluded and locally generated values dominate. Here immediacy prevails, even when it does violence to some of one's fundamental values. The Milgram experiments laid the groundwork for understanding this process, as later sections of this book will show.

One might argue that the Milgram findings deal only with a laboratory situation, and that they are not based on real life. However, there are real life corroborations of Milgram's findings. One example is a massacre that occurred in the Vietnam war. It became known to the general public when William Calley, a lieutenant in the U.S. Army, was accused of murdering unarmed, innocent old men, women, and children in the rural Vietnamese hamlet of My Lai in March 1968. During Calley's court martial the defense lawyer argued that Calley was following orders from higher-ranking officers, and that he was under severe stress at the time. The lawyer for the prosecution argued that Calley acted very much under his own discretion when ordering the Vietnamese to be killed and when he himself fired into the defenseless people huddled together in groups within the village. A jury of six fellow officers, including five Vietnam veterans, found Calley guilty of ordering and participating in the murders.

Although the results of the court martial are important, it is even more important to understand what went on inside Calley's head during the massacre. Calley himself provides a convincing picture of what when on in his head, although neither the prosecution nor his own lawyer seemed to believe him. What he said sounded so utterly simplistic and "ordinary" that few took him seriously. According to Calley one issue dominated the immediate context in which he found himself: to move his troops through the village and do it rapidly. To us, who are far removed from that day in March 1968, the order to move rapidly—and Calley had received a previous reprimand for not moving his men rapidly enough—may seem innocuous and trivial. To Calley it was very real and immediate. It was so real, in fact, that it dominated his actions to the extent of overruling any concern for the lives of Vietnamese citizens. Calley's perspective is illustrated in this exchange between Calley and the prosecuting attorney during the court martial:

> Prosecuting Attorney: How long did you fire into the ditch [where the Vietnamese were huddled]?
> Calley: I have no idea, Sir...
> P.A.: What at in the ditch?
> Calley: At the people in the ditch, Sir.
> P.A.: How many people in the ditch?
> Calley: I don't know, Sir...
> P.A.: What were these people doing as they were being fired upon?
> Calley: Nothing, Sir...
> P.A.: Were they being hit?
> Calley: I would imagine so, Sir.
> P.A.: Do you know?
> Calley: I don't know if they were being hit when I saw them, Sir.
> P.A.: Do you know if you hit any of them?
> Calley: No Sir, I don't.
> P.A.: How far away were you from them when you fired?
> Calley: The muzzle would have been five feet, Sir.
> P.A.: You didn't see the bullets impact?
> Calley: Not that I recall, no Sir.... My main thing was to go on, finish off these people as fast as possible and get my people out into position, Sir.
> P.A.: Why?
> Calley: Because that is what I was instructed to do, Sir, and I had been delayed long enough. I was trying to get out there before I got criticized again, Sir.[11]

In the immediate context Calley's foremost concern was to move his troops through the village very rapidly.

Calley was in charge of a platoon of soldiers, one of three such platoons engaged in sweeping through an area that was supposedly occupied by the enemy, the Viet Cong. Actually, there was no resistance whatever, because the enemy soldiers had previously withdrawn. Calley was under orders to proceed rapidly through the village, clearing it of all inhabitants. Apparently his platoon was slower than the others, and Calley had previously been reprimanded for slowness. In response to this reprimand Calley ordered that if the Vietnamese civilians could not be moved fast enough his men should kill them: He told a sergeant under him that if he could not "move" the people, he was to "waste" (i. e., kill) them. In short, Calley's horrendous deeds were carried out as he addressed himself to an innocuous (but, to him, very real) immediate problem—to avoid another reprimand for slowness.

In Calley's mind whatever interfered with moving his men rapidly was detrimental to this mission and had to be obliterated. In this case, the inhabitants could be seen as obstacles to getting through the village rapidly. He believed he did not have time to determine their potential to threaten his movement. He had to assume, he thought, that they were a hindrance. So, in his mind, it was necessary and justified to kill them. The low value he assigned to human life may strike us as appalling, but in Calley's scheme of thought the lives of Vietnamese civilians were a very minor aspect of his mission that day. Of course, addressing an immediate problem was not the only important factor in Calley's actions at My Lai. These other factors are described in Chapter 3.

THE DESIRE TO IGNORE EVIL

I began this book by saying that I tried to ignore the evil of the Holocaust for many years. I tried to shield myself. In a similar vein many American people tried to shield themselves about Vietnam in the 1960s and 1970s. During that time the daily television news routinely carried pictures of the latest atrocities in Vietnam. After repeatedly seeing these reports of killings, many Western viewers became emotionally numbed. People continued eating their evening meal while watching the latest pictures of atrocities on television. Similarly, responses to the Nazi Holocaust have reached the point of producing emotional exhaustion. Most of us have heard enough of the details to produce a lifetime's worth of emotional atrophy. This emotional exhaustion (or psychic numbing, as Robert Lifton calls it) is our defense against unbearable emotional assault. Our personal emotional system cannot stand being blinded by horrendous stimuli, so it puts up a curtain to cover our window to the world of evil.

However, extraordinary evil is real, and we cannot do away with it by putting up curtains to safeguard our senses. If we are to understand evil, and overcome it, we must pull aside the curtain. Yet we start with a handicap. Culturally produced sensibilities give us an aversion to exposing ourselves to extremes of evil. We do not want to see it or hear about it. Unfortunately, by closing our eyes and ears we are merely deceiving ourselves and giving evil the benefit of our ignorance. To overcome evil we must confront its realities. One of these realities is that people may engage in evil deliberately.

PEOPLE MAY DELIBERATELY ENGAGE IN EVIL ACTIVITIES

So far this book has painted a picture that makes evil seem accidental, a by-product of behavior that is not *intentionally* evil. Certainly, evil can happen accidentally, but there is also evil that is far from accidental; there is evil that is deliberate. There are occasions when persons do horrendous deeds *because* these deeds are horrendous. There are occasions when persons do evil *because* it is known to be evil.

For example, Dostoevski wrote about an incident of extraordinary evil that happened a hundred years ago, in another age, in another location; but it was real, and comparable activities take place in our own age.

In *The Brothers Karamazov*, Dostoevski wrote:

> a Bulgarian I met lately in Moscow, Ivan went on...told me about the crimes committed by the Turks and Circassians in Bulgaria through fear of a general uprising of the Slavs. They burned villages, murdered, outraged women and children, they

nailed their prisoners by the ears to the fences, left them till morning, and in the morning they hanged them—all sorts of things you can't imagine. People talk sometimes of bestial cruelty, but that's a great injustice and insult to the beasts; a beast can never be so cruel as a man, so artistically cruel. The tiger only tears and gnaws, that's all he can do. He would never think of nailing people by the ears, even if he were able to do it. These Turks took pleasure in torturing children, too; cutting the unborn child from the mother's womb, and tossing babies up in the air and catching them on the points of their bayonets before their mother's eyes. Doing it before the mother's eyes was what gave zest to the amusement. Here is another scene that I thought very interesting. Imagine a trembling mother with her baby in her arms, a circle of invading Turks around her. They've planned a game; they pet the baby, laugh to make it laugh. They succeed, the baby laughs. At that moment a Turk points a pistol four inches from the baby's face. The baby laughs, holds out its little hands to the pistol, and the Turk pulls the trigger in the baby's face and blows out its brains.[12]

Dostoevski did not want his readers to think that such cruelty was a uniquely Turkish disease. All societies have some of it. Dostoevski said:

I have Russian examples that are even better than the Turks. You know we prefer beating—rods and scourges—that's our national institution. Nailing ears is unthinkable for us, for we are, after all, Europeans. But the rod and scourge we have always with us and they cannot be taken away from us. Abroad now, they scarcely do any beating. Manners are more humane, or laws have been passed, so that they don't dare to flog men now. But they make up for it in another way just as national as ours...[13]

This is not accidental evil. It is deliberate evil. It is evil flaunted. As Kenneth Seeskin, a philosopher, said:

The killing [in the preceding passage] is not swift and impersonal but amusing and innovative: a grotesque form of self-expression. Despite what one might think after an initial reading of the passage, the person who plays with a baby in order to enjoy the slaughtering of it even more cannot be without a conscience. These are the actions of someone who understands only too well what human dignity is and takes pleasure in mocking it. In fact killing is symbolic. He has chosen to profane the tenderest and most sacred of living creatures and to do so in a manner designed to show the victim and everyone else that he is fully aware of the horror in what he is doing...[14]

If one could be sure that the flaunters of evil were sadists, suffering from psychopathology and so mentally unbalanced that they did not know right from wrong, one might almost be able to comprehend their evil. Even Hannah Arendt, in her effort to be objective about Eichmann, leaned in that direction. She claimed that Eichmann did not know right from wrong. But there was every indication that Eichmann was not mentally unbalanced. Arendt herself cited the psychiatric reports on Eichmann that said so. Similarly, psychiatrists found Lt. Calley to be quite sane. They affirmed that he could, indeed, distinguish right from wrong.

This points to yet another paradox: *Evil may be flaunted by people who know better.*

How can one explain the extraordinary level of evil that seemingly ordinary individuals may perpetrate? How can one explain the pursuit of evil when moral standards against such acts are known and are, to some extent at least, shared by those who carry out the evil? How can one explain the virtual courting of evil for its own sake? The answers seem to be contained in three phenomena I shall discuss in detail in Chapter 3, and describe briefly here.

Evil can be, and sometimes has been, *developed into a culture of cruelty*, a distinctive culture in its own right. As such it is systematically organized to reward individuals for their acts of cruelty: for being creative at inventing cruelties and for establishing a personal reputation for their particular version of cruelty. Here cruelty can be a macabre art form: one's creativity at inventing new forms of cruelty is socially recognized and rewarded. Here, too, cruelty can be a distinctive "economy," where one's credit rating depends on one's level of cruelty—the more cruel, the higher one's standing. By contrast, acts of kindness can lead to publicly declared bankruptcy, and in some situations the punishment for this bankruptcy is a death sentence.

Evil can be, and sometimes has been, *produced routinely, as an integral part of the operation of modern bureaucracy.* In some bureaucracies, such as Nazi extermination camps, the production of evil was the official mission of the bureaucracy. Here, merely being a bureaucratic functionary engaged the bureaucrat in routinely doing evil. However, in addition, bureaucrats often add to evil on their own initiative. On both counts, their contribution to evil can be enormous.

Evil can be, and sometimes has been, *produced in separate social contexts*. Evil is produced in the confines of a package of a number of items of valued behavior, which is organized under an all-embracing theme. That theme integrates and gives focus to behavior; it becomes a rider to all activities within the package, coloring all activities within that package; and it facilitates the outlook that everything outside the package can be ignored.

Such a rider helped to produce a context for evil in Nazi Germany. Hitler offered the German people a package that consisted of plans for revitalizing the German economy, recapturing German political glory that had been severely tarnished by defeat in the First World War, and racially "purifying" Germany. Hitler offered these items as separate issues under a unifying theme: the revived grandeur of Germany.

Hitler claimed that he, personally, was uniquely qualified to help restore Germany's grandeur. He was singularly attuned to Germany's destiny, its historic call to greatness. He, like Caesar and Alexander the Great, was to be the instrument for a nation's reaching its destiny. In this kind of myth great men, believed to be uniquely in touch with destiny, are held to be far above the level of ordinary humans. Hegel, a German philosopher who had helped establish this way of thinking, was sometimes quoted as saying that such superior persons "must trample down many an innocent flower, crush to pieces many objects in [their] path."[15] Hitler, like the legendary German hero Sigfried, "came to reawaken Germany to greatness, [and was a man] for whom morality, suffering and 'the litany of private virtues' was irrelevant."[16] Hitler was the implementor of the German people's destiny of greatness, and "anyone opposing them was flying in the face of the laws of Nature and Fate."[17]

This mythology meant that what was outside the Nazi package—namely, other German values, other concerns—had to be ignored. What Hitler offered the German people was a unifying theme, pursuit of national grandeur—with Hitler at the core, as its fundamental embodiment and leader—but with the German people sharing fully in the glory of it all while they participated in carrying out the Nazi package of programs. All economic, political, religious, and social life came to be pervaded by the rider of Hitler's grandiose theme. It fostered and permeated Nazi Germany.

The Nazi situation also illustrates the effects of a change of riders. Such a change may drastically alter an entire situation in which people live, even when much of their day-to-day behavior remains the same. In Germany many items of routine daily life remained the same between 1920 and 1933, yet life was thoroughly transformed by the emergence of the pursuit-of-grandeur rider, with a crucial turning point coming after Hitler's election as chancellor of Germany in 1933. As a result of the transformation, the German people took part in evil on a scale that would have been unthinkable to them before the emergence of the new rider. Yet much of the evil went unrecognized because so much of everyday life remained unchanged. In short, a new rider can entirely transform everyday living, while most ongoing activities remain unchanged.

This is the rider paradox: *Given a new rider to everyday living, little may change, but everything will be different.* In themselves, riders are neither good or bad. They are simply ways in which priorities from one sector of life intrude into, and dominate, other sectors of life—just as Hitler's personal grandiose heroics came to dominate much of the everyday life of the entire German people. Riders are linkage mechanisms, joining one sector of life to other sectors. And, finally, riders are organizing mechanisms: When a new rider prevails, a new set of priorities is imposed. Sometimes these new priorities create a context that legitimates extraordinary evil. To confront the evil it is necessary to recognize which riders are at work in that context and how they operate to facilitate evil.

The concepts outlined in this chapter form the basis for the understanding of how small, incremental steps, taken in our daily life, can have profound consequences; of how behavior is packaged and influenced by the riders that permeate it; and of how personal autonomy, one's ability to make independent decisions, can be used to contribute to horrendous evil. These ideas are examined next as they influence the actual practice of evil.

CHAPTER 2

Behavior Mechanisms at Work

Most of the persons who carried out the mass killings in this century were drawn from the ranks of ordinary citizens. These persons did not totally change when they participated in killings. They continued to be loyal citizens, doing what they thought was good for their country. In all likelihood the majority of the participants in some 10 million deaths during the Russian Revolution or some 20 million deaths in the Chinese Revolution did so out of a sense of loyalty to what they considered to be a grand cause.[1] They thought they were ushering in a new era of betterment for their country. The operators of the Nazi crematoria believed they were purifying Germany to make room for a greater and grander Germany.

In the administration of concentration camps the Nazis attempted to weed out the sadists and psychopaths from their ranks. "Ordinary" and "sane" officials were far more effective killers. They were more dependable instruments for carrying out the German state's policy of exterminating its opponents. Typically, these officials were not out for personal revenge or personal gain. They were loyal to what they regarded as a worthy cause, to a new golden age for their country. It may be hard to believe, but they often acted selflessly and loyally to their country.

Our century is not unusual in having large-scale killings carried out by well-intentioned citizens. Over the centuries, "the part played by crimes committed for personal motives is very small compared to the vast populations slaughtered in unselfish loyalty to a jealous god, country, or political system."[2] The well intentioned, the "good" people, have been most ardent participants in large-scale evil. Some of the human attributes we value most highly—selfless service to others, loyalty to one's country—are major ingredients in the most grotesque kinds of evil.

Do sane caring people engage in evil? Well, if by *evil* we mean the robbery and murder of one's neighbor, the rape of his wife, and the abuse of his children, the answer is No. The ordinary citizen does not do these things. If, on the other hand, we look at extraordinary levels of evil—at mass murder, reaching into the millions in the present century alone, and if we include massive abuse of large sectors of the world's population—then the answer is very different. Ordinary caring people do take part in extraordinary evil. And they do so with enthusiasm and innovativeness. Given sufficiently appealing circumstances, caring citizens will turn upon the designated enemy with passionate ferocity. In loyalty to a cause they will deprive that designated enemy of freedom and of life itself. To achieve it, in selfless dedication citizens will donate their own lives, and the lives of their children, doing so with the noblest of intentions.

We humans are not only meat-eating killers of other species, we are also highly uncompromising social animals. In sociological terms, we kill members of our own species to protect our favorite political system; we kill to protect our favorite religious system; we kill to protect our favorite economic system. In short, we kill for high social reasons. Stated differently, we live our personal lives under the sponsorship of specific social arrangements, and we guard these arrangements zealously. We are prepared to kill to protect the social arrangements under which we live. In moral terms, we kill for altruistic, not for selfish purposes. Why does this happen? Or, in more practical terms, *how* does it happen? What behavior mechanisms are at work?

INCREMENTAL PROCESSES

A large part of our daily life is filled with small, uneventful decisions. We ordinarily deal with today's problems today, tomorrow's problems tomorrow. Once in a while we make "big" decisions, but they are the exception rather than the rule. Usually we deal with small, immediate matters as they come along. Each event—deciding what to cook for today's dinner, deciding to take the car for an oil change today rather than next week—is seen "locally," without linking it to any very profound and great totality. Typically, such small events touch only a small part of the large social arrangements under which we exist, be it our national citizenship, our work and career, our religion, or our family life.

Hence the decision requires no great questioning of one's values, or the world in which we find ourselves. Such localized decisions are the increments in a way of life that is often fairly stable and uneventful. Each individual decision is part of the enactment of that way of life.

Yet through this type of localized incremental decision making the individual can readily become involved in profound evil, without recognizing that it is happening. The young American who was drafted into the army in the Vietnam era did not start out thinking that he might indiscriminately kill innocent men, women, and children. This is not what they told him at the induction center. Random killing came into some soldiers' life incrementally, step by step. Following the death of a close buddy or after seeing a horribly mutilated body of an American soldier who had been ambushed, our youthful, idealistic American soldier became less innocent. He might then, with a clear conscience set fire to a Viet Cong village, even when no enemy soldiers but only unarmed women and children were found. It might all happen within a day's incremental exchange of atrocities.

Incremental decisions often play a part in day-to-day living. In themselves they are neither good or evil. But they are a critical component in the process that can lead to extraordinary evil.

PACKAGES AND RIDERS

In the Vietnam war many atrocities were committed, and doubtless atrocities have been committed in other wars. But never before were atrocities brought home to Americans so immediately. During that war millions of Americans saw on the regular evening television news the most graphic reports of atrocities. In the confines of their homes, Americans saw sights that no human being should see, heard sounds that no human being should hear. It all became part of the American national diet: atrocities before dinner.

When journalists reporting from the field amplified the television scenes, it became clear that atrocities were being committed on both sides. Not only the enemy, but our own people—the "good" guys in the drama—were committing atrocities. How could this be? It was easily conceivable that the enemy might include individuals who were virtual monsters, capable of committing atrocities. But our own people? We knew better than that. We had learned from previous wars that soldiers, brought up in wholesome, humane families, could go off to war and kill and then return to wholesome, humane family life. Surely, we told ourselves, these soldiers, the fathers and grandfathers of the American soldiers in Vietnam, had not committed atrocities. And surely Americans who served in Vietnam were no different from their fathers and grandfathers.

Yet the atrocities were real. The pictures and sounds on the evening news were real. The stories written by journalists were real. These things happened. How could our people do such things?

The answer seems to be that, during the heat of battle, an individual soldier's priorities can become drastically rearranged. (This rearrangement may be temporary or permanent.)

There is every indication that the American soldier who killed innocent citizens in Vietnam retained the Western value that one should not kill innocent people. But in Vietnam this value sometimes played only a minor part among the soldier's guiding principles. On some occasions the prohibition against killing was subordinated to revenging the ambushing of a close friend or to other values within one's package of values. The Vietnam package of values was a rearranged version of the peacetime American values on which most soldiers were brought up. Not to kill still remained a powerful value in relation to fellow Americans—one does not kill Americans! But in relation to the Viet Cong it was decidedly subordinated to other values. The values had been repackaged.

Packaging can be seen as follows. At any one time, each of us has a number of different values. These values are the result of one's upbringing, one's learning and maturation process. Furthermore, not only do we have a number of different values, but at any one time these values are arranged in a definite order. Some things are more important than others. Some things can be achieved right away, while others must be held in abeyance. Some things can be neglected. Others have priority and must be tackled immediately. In short, at any one time, our values are unequal. They are organized—they are *packaged*—in definite ways.

In addition, packaged values are often influenced by forces that act as *riders* to the entire package. A rider places an imprint on every item within a package. In Vietnam, in the heat of military action, there was a pervasive rider that dominated the outlook of American soldiers. That rider was called *body count*. It demanded from the individual soldier, How many enemy soldiers have you killed? American units were evaluated on the basis of how many enemy soldiers they killed. Success was measured by the body count, which became the main criterion for judging military effectiveness. The body count was announced daily, keeping soldiers continually aware that it was being taken very seriously by the highest military officers. So pervasive was this attention to the body count that it became a rider to the ongoing activities of the individual soldier. It told the individual soldier that the first and foremost priority was to kill North Vietnamese soldiers; other considerations, other items in his package of values, were secondary. In many situations it was the dominant rider upon the individual soldier's package of values. It led to great emphasis on killing, regardless who was killed. (It also led to exaggerated and utterly fictitious reporting of killings.)

In Nazi Germany, Hitler carefully cultivated a rider that organized thought and action—much of the package—of the German people. The rider was Germany's "rightful" claim to grandeur and the "unfair" interference with that claim by Germany's enemies. One of Hitler's most effective symbols was the so-called Diktat of Versailles. After Germany lost the First World War, in 1918, the victorious Allies imposed a peace treaty, the Treaty of Versailles. The treaty ordered Germany to pay reparation money to the Allied countries, to give up certain territories Germany had captured, and to disarm most of its military forces, leaving it only with a token army, really a police militia.

The German people took this very hard. In particular, the disarming of Germany's military forces was seen as the most crushing and humiliating punishment of all. Many dreams of national glory were wrapped up in Germany's military forces. Disarmament meant an end to these dreams.

Hitler took full advantage of these crushed dreams. Over and over, in speech after speech, he hurled forth the phrase *Diktat of Versailles* to keep alive the German fury at the Allies. Masterfully, Hitler used Versailles as a symbol for rallying the people to his program: to rearm Germany, to regain Germany's "stolen" territory, to get Germany ready to act on the quest for ever greater national glory. Versailles served as a reminder of injury to the rider, German grandeur, that organized German aspirations under Hitler's priorities. As Hitler hammered home the Versailles theme, it left its imprint on the thoughts and deeds of the German population. Little in German national life remained untouched by the sense of national shame and fury. All of German national life, its total package of values, was colored by this rider. It arranged the German people's priorities. It taught them what was important and what was not important within their package of values. It taught them, above all, that Germans could regain their sense of self-respect only when Germany regained her grandeur which, in turn, required full implementation of Hitler's package of policies, which included political and military adventurism and unlimited anti-Semitism.[3]

THE QUESTION OF AUTONOMY:
THE CUNNING OF GOVERNMENTS AND
THE CONTRIBUTIONS OF CITIZENS

Prewar Germany is instructive in an additional way. It shows how citizens contribute to making the dreams of their leaders become a reality.

I became aware of this from personal experience. I was born into a Jewish family in a small village in the north Bavarian part of Germany. When the Nazi regime began its harassment of Jews in the 1930s our non-Jewish neighbors said, after each incident: "There is nothing we could do about it. We are just little people. It's the government."

I visited the village thirty years after most members of my family and of the other Jewish families from the village were murdered in death camps. The villagers again said, "There is nothing we could do about it. We are just little people. It's the government." I am not paraphrasing. These were the exact words (in German) announced once again. The villagers' view of themselves and their world was remarkably stable.

Yet some little people, in some little villages, did do something about it. They hid some of these hounded people. They fed some of these hounded people. They helped some of these hounded people escape.

During the visit to my village I found out that there had been one exception to the pattern of passively leaving Jews to the evil deeds of the Nazi government: A lone woman stood by Jews. She brought them food. She talked with them. She did not join in the distancing by the rest of the villagers. But she was not able to save anyone or offer much protection. She said to me, concerning the Nazis, "what they did was not right." And she wept.

Despite such exceptional human beings, the Nazi-German government achieved its objectives of carrying out massive evil because it had the help of a multitude of "the little people," who paid their taxes, sent their sons to the front, and closed their eyes to the savaging of innocent people in their midst.

Are people merely the victims of their government? During the Nuremberg trials of Nazi war criminals it was customary for the accused to say that he was merely following orders established by the government. The accused claimed they were loyal, law-abiding citizens. When faced with an order by one's government one had to obey. Army officers, in particular, invoked the idea of *duty*. It was one's duty, sometimes they used the term *sacred duty*, to obey one's government.

Even my fellow villagers in Bavaria believed that it was their duty to obey the government. The government was not merely infinitely bigger and stronger than "the little people" of the village, the villagers also owed a duty to the government. On the basis of this duty they did not question the government's policy of uprooting and murdering Jews who had lived in their midst for centuries. They also did not question the government's right to conscript the young men, their sons, for military service in the war.

When fully one-half of the village's young men did not return from the war—attesting to the fact that uneducated, backwoods people make excellent cannon fodder—they still did not question their duty to the government. Instead, they erected a plaque in the village square. It was dedicated to the memory of the dutiful obedience of those who did not return. On the plaque is listed the name of each of the village sons who perished in the Second World War. The village thereby remembers, in love and respect, how these sons gave the final measure of devotion to duty.

To me, the sons of the village who perished were my classmates and their older brothers. They had tormented me because I was Jewish. They had broken our dog's leg because he was a Jewish dog. They had made going to school a daily nightmare for me. Then they went off to war, in which they would inflict more torment. In turn, they, their families and their village reaped the harvest of the ultimate torment: death in their own midst.

Were the village sons innately evil? Or were they fairly ordinary sorts of people, who were awash in evil, tormenting Jews when it was a sporting thing to do, going off to war to kill when it was one's duty to do so?

I think they were not innately evil. In many ways they were ordinary people, but their actions were mightily evil. They contributed to their government's pursuit of extraordinary evil, and they did so eagerly. They were not reluctantly evil. They needed little coercing by their government. The remaining villagers, the parents and the sisters of the soldiers, also contributed to evil. They did so by their silence and by their active support of the government and its policies.[4]

How cunning are governments? How do governments obtain the support of their citizens? The Nazi-German government had power over its citizens. With that power at its disposal it could brutally enforce virtually every one of its demands upon the villagers. But usually it did not need to use brute force. In the name of duty the government could, and did, demand sacrifices from its citizens. The citizens responded, including donation of the ultimate sacrifice, the lives of their sons. When this ultimate sacrifice was accepted by the government, when the sons died, the citizens did not question the need for such a sacrifice. They did not turn against their government, in consternation and fury—instead, they sanctified the sacrifice. They erected a plaque.

To be regarded as legitimate, governments need the help of their citizens. It is the citizens who erect the plaques. It is the citizens who do the sanctifying. *They* bring the fresh flowers to the plaque. *They* stop by the plaque, on their way to and from work, to look at the names of their sons. First, they do so in a spirit of stricken grief and sorrow. Then, over time, their sentiment turns to pride and a measure of satisfaction in the sons who did their duty for a great cause. They thereby sanctify their sons and the policies of the government.

Without such sanctifications by the citizens, without citizens' donating their support for policies, governments are hollow shells. *The cunning of governments consists of getting their citi-*

zens to attribute sanctity to government policies, no matter how evil they may be. Coercion alone will not accomplish this, not even in totalitarian countries like Russia before Gorbachev. Government propaganda alone will not accomplish this (although some governments have developed brainwashing to a fine art). Nor is it a matter of leadership alone: Leaders need followers. Followers donate legitimacy to leaders. They do so by using their own autonomy to give or to deny support to the leader. "Leaders" without followers end up in mental hospitals.

When the villagers said they were powerless, "little people" they did not give an accurate description of the support they contributed to the Nazi movement. Throughout Germany the "little people," by the millions, gave both passive and active support to Nazism. Passively, they failed to interfere with the Nazi storm troopers and hooligans who ransacked Jewish homes in the early years of Nazism; and they failed to try to subvert the highly organized extermination campaign when it hit their own neighborhood in the latter years of Nazism. Actively, they collaborated in the Nazi cause by freely joining the Nazi party, by helping to enact its package of programs, by sanctifying its actions, and by donating the lives of their own sons.

The cunning of governments operates by harvesting the contributions of their citizens. The citizens, for their part, have much autonomy to decide what sort of contributions they will make.

A crucial point is how one uses one's autonomy: how one uses the choices one has available. Often we believe we have no autonomy, no freedom to choose, when in fact we have a great amount of autonomy. Even when one lives under an authoritarian government, as in Nazi Germany, or when one finds oneself in a military situation, as American soldiers did in Vietnam, the issue is not whether one has choices, but how one uses the choices one has available.

* * *

Behavior mechanisms used in ordinary day-to-day living lend themselves to a humane, productive and good life, but they also lend themselves to active contribution to monstrous acts. The next chapter illustrates this process by contrasting and comparing the ordinary day-to-day life of a humane modern physician with the lives and actions of other ordinary, but evil, men.

CHAPTER 3

Some Faces of Evil

The first face is not evil at all. It belongs to an American physician who is an exemplary humane human being. It is a face whose owner accepts a rider that provides a safeguard against evil. Without this safeguard some of his behavior could be rudiments for horrendous evil.

The other three faces are those of a university medical researcher who became an SS physician at Auschwitz; a professional administrative bureaucrat who headed Auschwitz; and an American career officer who served in Vietnam. These last three practiced evil. All three teach us lessons about ordinary behavior being used to produce extraordinary evil.

A HUMANE AMERICAN PHYSICIAN

"What I look forward to, when I get up in the morning, is seeing some disease."

These are the words of a hospital pathologist, Dr. Doe (not his real name, of course).[1] Dr. Doe works in a medium-sized hospital, where he is in charge of clinical laboratory services. Technicians working under him carry out a large number of blood and urine tests every day. Dr. Doe examines all tissues removed from patients during operations, studying them under a microscope, and he performs the autopsies on patients who have died. His findings from the clinical tests, from the examination of tissues and from the autopsies are sent to the clinician treating the current patient or who treated the deceased patient.

Dr. Doe has a reputation for being serious, honest, humane, and rigorous in his work. Among his colleagues in the hospital and among pathologists in other hospitals, he is held in the high-

45

est esteem. When it comes to medical matters, I would not have the slightest qualms about entrusting my life to him.

Yet Dr. Doe says he dislikes having to deal with patients. He has as little contact with them as he can. He says that patients, and particularly their families, bother him when they ask a lot of questions. He prefers to avoid them. Instead, Dr. Doe loves to study disease processes. They are his passion.

One morning, during the time I was with him, Dr. Doe was in an unusual, highly animated state. Generally he was very quiet and reserved. This morning he was bursting with fervor. It turned out that he had solved a major medical riddle. Four months earlier a patient had undergone an operation and the tissue removed at that time proved to be extremely difficult to diagnose. Dr. Doe sent samples of the tissue to other pathologists in various parts of the country. None had been able to formulate a diagnosis. Now Dr. Doe himself managed to make the diagnosis. The patient had a very rare form of cancer.

Every physician who came to Dr. Doe's laboratory that morning heard Dr. Doe tell about the triumphant success of the diagnosis. Over and over, he told how he had finally hit upon the answer. However these physicians, all clinicians, remained quiet, in fact they were downright glum. They gave no sign of sharing Dr. Doe's jubilation.

The truth of the matter was that the patient had died six weeks earlier. As far as the clinicians were concerned, that was the end of the battle, because their foremost concern was keeping the patient alive. In contrast, Dr. Doe's foremost concern was knowing what was wrong with the patient, what disease he had. He was not happy about the patient's death, but he was exceedingly pleased about discovering the cause of his death. (Of course, Dr. Doe's success with this patient might help future patients. A future patient with the same symptoms would doubtless be diagnosed rapidly.)

Dr. Doe has a great deal of commitment to one aspect of medicine, research. At heart he is a research scientist, and perhaps a detective. But in reality he is a practicing physician. Every day scores of patients are seriously influenced by his medical judgment. He may not like dealing with patients, but he does deal with patients (and he does so in a courteous and kindly manner). He sees a few every week. And he gets involved in the personal side of the practice of medicine indirectly, in terms of what he communicates to the patient's own physician. Internists and surgeons urge Dr. Doe to be clear-cut in his diagnoses, so that they, in turn, can be clear-cut in the advice they give to patients and their families. (One pathologist, not Dr. Doe, regularly gives clinicians two diagnoses for each patient: one, a "simplistic" version, to give to patients; another one, a "scientific" version, to spell out fully the doubts and uncertainties actually present.)

In short, Dr. Doe is involved in a broad range of activities. He has a serious personal commitment to some of them—to the scientific ones, especially—and very little to others. However, he cannot escape those to which he has little commitment. Like it or not, he has to get involved with patients. He considers himself primarily a scientist rather than a healer, but being a practicing physician makes him a healer nonetheless.

Dr. Doe may not be so very unusual. We live in a fairyland if we believe that every physician is committed to healing, that every teacher is committed to teaching, that every soldier is committed to fighting, that every mother is committed to mothering. For example, Sylvia Ashton Warner, a much-honored teacher, wrote in her autobiography (published in 1979) that she did not like teaching, that she had no real commitment to teaching.

In a study of student nurses in the 1960s, Harry W. Martin and I found that some young women chose their nursing career in a series of steps, *none* of which involved a commitment to nursing. Typically, approaching the end of high school, some of them had simply not made a decision about what sort of career they wanted. In the absence of a work-career commitment, they went to nursing school because a good friend had gone there or because it seemed a good place to catch an eligible doctor. By going to nursing school they were realistically tackling an immediate goal that confronted them at that time, such as finding a husband. That goal had nothing to do with nursing.

After beginning the nursing school program, students were very likely to complete it, because it would be costly to drop out and start over in something else. Even if the student nurse did not develop a commitment to nursing, she was likely to complete the program once she had become involved in it.

In short, a person may go through a period of full professional training, and then enter the profession, such as nursing, without a professional and personal commitment to that profession! Furthermore, just because a person works in an occupation, it does not mean that he or she has a full commitment to that occupation. An individual who failed to get through medical school, then transferred and successfully completed dental school may still be committed to medicine while practicing dentistry. One may then go to one's grave considering oneself to be a failed physician.

For most of us the situation is not quite so harsh. Perhaps like Dr. Doe we have a strong commitment to some aspects of our occupation and little commitment to the rest of it, yet we are involved in the full range of activities required by that occupation. There is nothing unusual or abnormal in this. We may end up in occupations to which we are not fully committed, just as we may end up living in a place to which we have no great commitment or participate in causes to which we have no great commitment, often as the result of a series of small, incremental decisions. Individually, each incremental decision may not have envisaged our current situation, but together, cumulatively, they led to our participation in our current situation.

Viewed another way, one's work imposes a whole package of obligations, but one may sense a commitment to only a few items within that package, just as Dr. Doe had a commitment mainly to research but found himself with obligations to a variety of patient-care activities. Despite his commitment to only a few items, he carried out the total package of obligations, and did so thoroughly and conscientiously.

On a larger scale—and in a far more dangerous way—the Hitler era had Germans carrying out the total Nazi package of programs, including the economic revitalization of the country, a return to Germany having greater power internationally, and racial "purification" within Germany. After the war many Germans claimed to have had a commitment to only one or two of the items of the Nazi package and that they had been going along with the rest of the package grudgingly. This may well have been true. Yet "going along" often meant making substantial contributions to items within a package to which the individual had little personal commitment. Among the Germans, "going along" meant participating in items such as murderous anti-Semitism by individuals who were not very anti-Semitic, and participating in awesome military adventurism by persons who, personally, did not consider themselves militarists.

Admittedly, it seems illogical to say that a person may make substantial contributions in areas to which one has no personal commitment. It seems even more illogical to say that these contributions may surpass those of the "committed" person. But in reality this can happen. To see how this is possible we need only return to Hitler's Germany, where there was no question that one of the most fanatical anti-Semites was Julius Streicher, the editor of the newspaper *Der Stuermer*. Anti-Semitism was probably the centerpiece of Streicher's life, the most fundamental of all his commitments. Under him *Der Stuermer* poured forth a steady stream of the vilest propaganda against Jews. Streicher displayed his anti-Semitism openly and publicly. In contrast, Adolf Eichmann claimed that he was not an anti-Semite. If we take Eichmann at his word, that his real commitment was to his career and not to the murder of Jews, we are still left with the fact that his anti-Semitic deeds were very real and very awesome. In their direct destructive impact on the lives of Jews they far surpassed those of Streicher, the man whose primary commitment was to anti-Semitism.

In short, doing evil deeds does not require a primary or open commitment to doing evil. This indicates a critical dimension in the practice of evil: *People can be recruited to do evil without being asked for a commitment to evil, and yet be expected to carry out evil deeds.*[2]

There is another side to the packaging phenomenon. In addition to actively practicing what one does not believe, one may *not* practice what one *does* believe. What one does believe may be dominated and overlaid by other components of one's package. (This feature was crucial to the behavior of Rudolf Hoess, which is discussed later in this chapter.) Some beliefs may stay dormant for long periods of time, but remain available for activation under suitable conditions. In the service of evil, for example, long-dormant prejudices and hatreds can be activated under suitable conditions when many thought that these prejudices and hatreds had been eradicated long ago.

In this section Dr. Doe showed that one can participate in an entire package of activities, even those to which one has little or no commitment. In Dr. Doe's case, all the activities were benign, since they all related to giving medical care. But in cases where parts of a package of activities are thoroughly evil, as in the Nazi extermination program, people can participate in evil without a commitment to evil. This opens up a large reservoir of potential participants in evil. One person selected from this reservoir was Dr. Kremer, a highly educated German university-based research physician. He was not committed to killing innocent human beings. Yet he became an enthusiastic member of the medical staff of Auschwitz, where killing innocent human beings was an everyday occurrence. There, at Auschwitz, he did participate in killing innocent human beings.

AN SS PHYSICIAN

The case of Dr. Johann Paul Kremer, an SS physician, will show how the content of a behavior package can become utterly corrupted, leading an individual to willingly participate in evil. It will show that the dominant rider to that package can be crucial in making the individual a willing participant in all the activities demanded by that package, even those he first regards as abhorrent.

The Kremer case also illustrates that the medical world contains the rudiments of evil. Some of its most humane activities are but an incremental step away from great evil. Ordinarily, the prevailing medical rider, about the sanctity of all human life, prevents this step from being taken. But a new rider can completely change the picture, resulting in evil of a horrendous kind.

Dr. Kremer was a physician who had taught and carried out research at a university before serving in the Auschwitz concentration camp as an SS physician. Like Dr. Doe, Kremer had a personal commitment to medical research, and like Dr. Doe he found himself in a work context that required some activities he did not like, but in which he became involved. However, unlike Dr. Doe's work context, Kremer's context included the most gruesome deeds imaginable, and he participated in these gruesome deeds with enthusiasm. And after doing so, subsequent to his release from prison after the war, he returned to his university. He wanted to resume his university career as though his commitment to medicine was unblemished.

Kremer, who was born in 1884, was doubtless one of the older SS officers to serve at Auschwitz. He had gained a reputation as a researcher in genetics. He was a professor (to be more precise, he was a *dozent*, roughly the equivalent of a lecturer at an American university) at the University of Muenster.

The Nazi movement had attracted many prominent persons, including a number of university faculty members. Kremer was one of them. He joined the Nazi party in July 1932; possibly he was the first person to do so at his university. He joined the SS in 1935.

Kremer's research focused on human heredity. He claimed that he had found evidence that traumatic injuries to parents produced changes that were transmitted to their offspring, allowing induction of hereditary changes. This idea was very attractive to the Nazis, as they wanted to create a master race. Problems of heredity, particularly deliberate genetic changes, fascinated many Nazis. (Himmler, the SS chief, was very interested in genetics.)

Which came first? Did Kremer begin as a Nazi and then adjust his research to suit Nazi ideology? Or did his research interest come first and then draw him to Nazism because of its similar views on racial matters? We will probably never answer this question. At any rate, Kremer's colleagues at the university did not embrace his research findings with wild enthusiasm. And Kremer, for his part, felt that his work was not properly appreciated by his fellow professors, who were lukewarm about it. This attitude came to a head in the university's resistance to granting him his fondest wish, a professorial chair in genetics. This goal eluded him to the end of his days.

However, the Nazis honored Kremer for his work, and Kremer, in turn, gave the Nazis the full measure of his devotion. He was assigned to Auschwitz for about three months, and then he returned to his university. Kremer kept a detailed diary covering his service at Auschwitz.[3]

The diary is an astounding document. In it Kremer shows himself to be the most pedantic, most officious, most status-hungry of bureaucrats. Were it not for the bizarre fact that it covers Kremer's encounter with and participation in grotesquely evil deeds, one might use the diary to dismiss Kremer as a buffoon, suitable for a leading role in a comic opera and for very little else. However, Kremer's evil deeds were real and in its perverse way, the diary is a gem.

The diary notes that Kremer volunteered his services to the SS early in the war. He was then fifty-seven years old. In August 1941, he was ordered to the Dachau concentration camp for military training. He was assigned to the surgery unit. His diary describes the types of operations being performed there, the food, the "good beer," the "beautiful scenery," the "wonderful weather," a visit to the zoo. He does *not* mention the prisoners.

In September he was transferred to another camp. There he describes a visit to the cinema and work on his scientific writing. He gives a very detailed statement of his experiences, itemizing his purchases of food and a pair of riding boots. He always indicates the rank of the person with whom he is associating. And, again, there is no mention of the prisoners. After the period of training Kremer returned to his university.

In the diary Kremer reserved his most tender expression of feelings for his canary. When it died, Kremer wrote: "Haenschen [the canary] ceased to suffer at 2 p. m. I was extremely sorry, as I had been so used to this poor little fellow, always so lively. Cremation..."[4] No human being receives such warm sentiments from him. (Kremer had been married in 1920. Some months after the wedding he and his wife separated. In 1942, during his service at Auschwitz, the divorce became final. Kremer expressed great relief and joy at that time.)

In August 1942 Kremer was ordered to "Concentration Camp Auschwitz to replace a surgeon who had been taken sick."[5] He arrived on August 30. On August 31 he remarked about the "tropical climate" and the "excellent food."[6]

> September 2, 1942:
>
> Was present for the first time at a special action [mass execution, usually by gassing] at 3 a.m. By comparison Dante's Inferno seems almost a comedy. Auschwitz is justly called an extermination camp.[7] [That day 957 Jews had arrived from France. All but twelve men and twenty-seven women were immediately killed by gassing.]

In the gassing procedures, a physician supervised preparation of the gas pellets, and after the gassing, the physician would certify that the victims were indeed dead. It is not clear whether, on that first day, Kremer was involved in these activities. The selection process, choosing who would die and who would live, was also usually administered by a physician.

September 5, 1942:

...was present at a special action in the women's camp, the most horrible of horrors...the military surgeon [a colleague] is right when he said to me today that we are located in the *anus mundi* [anus of the world]...[8]

September 6, 1942:

Today an excellent Sunday dinner...[lists the delectable dishes]...In the evening at 8 o'clock attended another special action outdoors.[9]

September 9, 1942:

This morning received word from my solicitor [that Kremer's divorce was now final]...I see light again, the black curtain hanging over my life has been lifted...later was present as physician at the flogging of eight camp inmates [presumably he had to certify at which point the flogging would be lethal] and at one execution by shooting with a small calibre gun. Got soap flakes and two cakes of soap.... In the evening present at a special action.[10] [That evening 893 Jews arrived from Westerbork in Holland. All but fifty-nine men and fifty-two women were immediately killed by gassing.]

September 17, 1942:

Have ordered a casual coat from the Clothes Distribution Office [of the SS in Berlin.] Tailor's measurements: down to the waist 48, whole length 133, half of the back 22, down to the elbow 51, whole length of sleeve 81, chest measurement 107, waist 100, set 124. Have enclosed coupons for the coat, as part of my uniform. Together with Dr. Meyer today visited the women's camp at Birkenau.

September 20, 1942:

This Sunday afternoon from 3 p. m. till 6 p. m. I listened to a concert of the prisoners' band in glorious sunshine; the bandmaster was a conductor of the Warsaw State Opera. Eighty musicians. Roast pork for dinner, baked tench for supper.

September 23, 1942:

This night was present at the sixth and seventh special actions. Obergruppenfuehrer Pohl [wearing] suit arrived at the Waffen SS club-house [officer's club] in the morning. The sentry at the door presented arms before me for the first time. At 8 o'clock in the evening supper in the [residence of] Obergruppenfuehrer Pohl, a truly festive meal. We had baked pike, as much of it as we wanted, real coffee, excellent beer and sandwiches.[11]

October 6, 1942:
  Obersturmfuehrer Entres met with an accident on his motorcycle; I dressed his injuries; Commandant Hoess fell from his horse....[12]

These are examples of the routine of an SS physician's life at Auschwitz. *After his first two diary entries expressing horror about the murderous deeds, Kremer never again mentioned a sense of horror.* Step by step, incrementally, he became used to it. He routinely placed mention of taking part in "special actions" alongside the things that really counted for him: the joys of eating, associating with high-ranking officers, being saluted by underlings, getting a tailor-made uniform. What Robert Lifton calls the *medicalization of killing* became part of his comfortable way of life, filled with daily satisfactions. For Kremer this life had its own compelling immediacy. Here the outside world's moral code and the ethics of the medical profession were merely a distant glimmer. They did not penetrate into Kremer's current situation.

Kremer's involvement in medical evil was probably similar to that of the other SS physicians who served at Auschwitz. But Kremer, the researcher, had a specialty. He was interested in how starvation produced changes in the human body, and at Auschwitz he seized the opportunity to study the effects of starvation.

For his research Kremer wanted *lebensfrisches* human tissue. The English language has no adequate way of translating the term *lebensfrisch*. Perhaps this is one form of brutality we have not yet assimilated into English-speaking ways of thinking. The closest approximation to *lebensfrisch* is "living fresh," or human tissue that is still in a living state. Kremer made arrangements to obtain this tissue.[13]

Kremer chose likely candidates for his research from among prisoners who were already earmarked for death because of their starvation. He reports:

  The patient was put on the dissecting table while he was still alive. I then approached the table and put several questions to the man as to such details which pertained to my researches. For instance, I asked what his weight had been before the arrest, how much weight he had lost since then, whether he took medicine, etc. When I had collected my information the orderly approached the patient and killed him with an injection in the vicinity of the heart. As far as I knew only phenol injections were used. Death was instantaneous after the injection. I myself never made any lethal injections.[14]

How could Kremer ignore the medical ethics that prohibit killing people? How could he, a physician, abide the fact that "the orderly approached the patient [note the use of the word *patient*, a concept that has some sanctity in the medical profession] and killed him..."? To understand Kremer's action one must realize that he did not invent this kind of research from scratch. Instead, he used his own discretion, his own autonomy, to go merely one incremental step beyond two well-respected realities in medical research: (1) the professional researcher's focus on discovery, and (2) the use of animals for experimental purposes.

First, as a professional researcher, Kremer's professional life was geared to discovering new knowledge. (Remember Dr. Doe, who looks forward to seeing some disease when he wakes up in the morning! He does not enjoy seeing people suffer from disease, but he does enjoy encountering disease in order to discover something new about it.) A successful researcher is someone who discovers new knowledge, not someone who merely reiterates what is already known. *Discovery* is the focus of the researcher's career. *Discoveries* determine one's career rewards. *Discovering* permeates one's thinking.

The pursuit of discovery requires inventiveness—doing something that others have not done—particularly in one's research methods. Some Nobel Prize-winning scientists earned their reward not for discovering new knowledge, but for discovering new methods for discovering new knowledge. Discovering new *methods*, itself, is a highly valued goal in the world of the research scientist.

For Kremer, the use of human subjects was a new method. For him it was fascinating to use human beings because one could extract information from humans for which animals could not provide answers. One could, for example, ask them about their past behavior.

Auschwitz gave Kremer the autonomy to use humans in any way he wished. Nazi propaganda laid the groundwork when it asserted that the Jews (and Gypsies and other victims) were really subhumans. The Nazis held that these people may have been fully human for medical purposes, but they were not really fully human "racially." This caveat took care of any qualms raised by a Nazi-party physician's conscience. From then on, medically and scientifically, the Nazi ideology offered these physicians a unique opportunity to innovate research *methods*.

Second, animals are used for many purposes in modern laboratory research. For example, they are used to test new drugs before these drugs are used on humans. Often an animal's life is sacrificed to yield knowledge that may be of use in human medicine. In fact, hundreds of thousands of laboratory animals are killed each day. Animal sacrifice is a routine research procedure, and the fact that the animal is a living creature is given very little *moral* consideration. (Although it does weigh on the methods of sacrifice chosen. Humane methods are usually sought.)

Kremer's description of his research—how he chose research subjects based on scientific criteria, namely signs of starvation—is strikingly like a report on animal research. In its tone, in its exclusive focus on "scientific" facts, it might as well be a report on research using rabbits. In its style and format it is utterly in keeping with ongoing animal research, where living creatures are routinely killed to yield some new knowledge. One can well imagine that for Kremer it was but a small, incremental step to go from research that used animals to research that used humans as subjects.

Although it is true that scientists are always looking for new methods, and these are often rewarded and publicly acclaimed, there are limits to the kinds of innovations permitted. Each science operates within a particular perspective (or "paradigm" as the philosopher Thomas Kuhn calls it) that specifies for the scientists in a discipline the general consensus as to which methods are accepted, and regarded as legitimate, and which methods are clearly ruled out as illegitimate. In present-day medical research there is consensus that human beings are not to be used as subjects when their life is endangered by the research.

Yet this is not always clear-cut. For instance, doctors may try out experimental drugs, whose exact effects are not fully understood, as a medication of last resort, when all other efforts to save the patient have failed. Here the stated aim is to save the patient rather than to test a drug. In reality, however, the physician may believe that the patient will surely die. By giving the drug to the patient the physician may obtain some valuable information about the drug, even if its contribution to that patient's survival is marginal, at best. In the same manner, Kremer claimed that he chose "patients" for his research when these persons were already earmarked for death. Here, again, there is but a small, incremental step between the medication-of-last-resort research and Kremer's own research.

Scientists *do not* use humans in the same expendable way they use laboratory animals. Although a researcher might wish one could test a particular drug on humans, even when its characteristics are not fully known, one does not ordinarily go against the prevailing values of one's fellow scientists by testing the drug on humans. One does not do so because one shares one's discipline's values and one fears retribution if one violates existing values. If one violates these values one faces public disgrace and loss of one's license to engage in research or to practice medicine.

In contrast, a "scientist" like Kremer was not going against the prevailing values. As already discussed, the Nazis had laid the groundwork by declaring that Jews and certain other categories of people were subhuman—people who did not really deserve to live, who were a race apart form the pure Nordic Germans. This constituted the critical rider that enabled Kremer to equate research on humans with research on animals.

Furthermore, long before he went to Auschwitz, Kremer was a "marginal man" in his professional work and in his university. Much of his research was regarded with skepticism, if not scorn, by his colleagues. He was not promoted to high rank. He was involved in many fights with his colleagues. His willingness to join the Nazi movement early on also suggests that he was not well integrated into the traditional mainstream of the academic-scientific community. (This point is of limited importance, though, as some respected scientists also joined the Nazi movement.)

A marginal man is very likely to challenge "respectable people's" values. If he is a scientist, his marginality is likely to show up in his scientific work, especially in his methods. Because he does not have his colleagues' respect, his colleagues' scorn holds no threat. His thinking is that, if his colleagues do not reward him, why should he adhere to the limitations they impose on subjects and methods of research?

* * *

After the war a Polish court sentenced Kremer to death for his research activities. But due to his advanced age, the sentence was reduced to ten years in prison. Following his release, in 1958, Kremer returned to Germany. He regarded himself as a martyr, a person who was wrongly prosecuted. But his colleagues at the university did not see it this way, and they stripped him of his doctor's degree. Kremer died in the 1960s.

In summary, Kremer was a passionate scientist, who lived amid and for the research scientist's distinctive package of values, which is permeated by a basic rider: the quest for discovery. This much Kremer shared with many other scientists. But Kremer, the individual, went a crucial incremental step beyond the limitations ordinarily accepted by scientists. He used his autonomy to devise abhorrent methods of discovery that brought him into the mainstream of evil.[15]

The Thin Line Between Evil and Good: A Comparison of Dr. Doe and Dr. Kremer

Dr. Doe, the humane American research-minded physician and Dr. Kremer, the German university scientist who turned into an SS enthusiast, had much in common. In their work life, medical research—the quest for new knowledge about human disease processes—held a place of very high importance. For both of them medical research was an all-consuming passion. When Dr. Doe says that what he looks forward to when he gets up in the morning is seeing some disease, he is giving us access to the passionate life of the professional researcher. When Dr. Kremer sees the concentration camp as a grand opportunity to do research he was never able to do before (free of the humane restrictions against deliberate killing of human beings), we should not let our sense of abhorrence get in the way of recognizing that, for this researcher, it really did seem to be a grand opportunity to do research. To the passionate researcher, one's research work defines much of one's life. It defines how one sees oneself as a person and what one has to contribute to the world.

Beyond sharing a passion for medical research, the two physicians shared many of the viewpoints and behaviors of the professional medical researcher: starting from extensive knowledge of human physiology and biochemical processes, to special interest in some specific medical problems, to carefully practiced ways of observing and recording biochemical changes while using a variety of experimental techniques.

In summary, the passion for doing research by the two physicians, itself, is a *package* of behavior skills, values, and attitudes toward their work. For both of these research-minded physicians this package has similar content, with the demand for discovery serving as rider that organizes and justifies the entire package. For both physicians the passion for medical research was a centerpiece in their professional life.

For Dr. Doe, research mindedness produced his ambivalence toward patients. He was far more actively concerned with his patients' diseases than their personal needs. He saw having occasional contact with patients as an inconvenient but necessary fact of life, because it enabled him to combine a clinical medical practice (from which he derived his income, but few "interesting" relationships with clinical colleagues) with research (from which he derived no income, but much professional satisfaction, including gratifying professional interactions with fellow pathologists in other hospitals).

Dr. Kremer carried his research mindedness a crucial incremental step further. He indulged it to the extent of treating concentration camp inmates as guinea pigs, as animals that can be killed at will to produce more medical knowledge. The very common practice, in medical research, of treating laboratory animals as expendable, whose lives have value only to produce information that will help us conquer human disease, is also part of the research passion.

It is clear that much of the day-to-day behavior of the two research-minded physicians was similar. Much of their commitment to medical research, as a central factor in their lives, was similar. Yet there was also a world of difference between Dr. Doe and Dr. Kremer. They accepted two very different riders from the society in which they lived. These riders altered the two researchers' packages drastically.

Specifically, Dr. Kremer fully accepted the Nazi ideology as a rider to his professional life. (Remember Dr. Kremer, and many other scientists, accepted the Nazi ideology voluntarily and willingly.) This meant that Jews and Gypsies, and any other category the German government chose to designate, were classified as subhuman. And subhumans were regarded as expendable, vermin to be destroyed. They could be used as guinea pigs for research. They had the advantage over guinea pigs in that, for medical purposes, their bodies were like those of other human beings. Yet, like guinea pigs, there were no moral scruples against using them for research. All this was made possible because Dr. Kremer accepted the rider that defined the Auschwitz inmates as subhumans.

By contrast, Dr. Doe fully accepted a social ethic emphasizing the sanctity of all human life as a rider to his professional work. This ethic derives from the mainstream of Western religious, political, and philosophical traditions. As a rider to his professional work it set severe limits on his scientific research. Human beings could not be used as guinea pigs for research.

In short, the dividing line between good and evil is thin. Both doctors have a commitment to medical research, with its fundamentally *good* objective of discovering ways to improve human health by learning more about human illness and defects. They share commitment to a broad range of behavior needed to accomplish this objective. They differ only in one ingredient. Dr. Kremer accepts and Dr. Doe rejects a rider that defines certain people as subhuman. Thereby the immediate context in which they find themselves is defined totally differently. Dr. Doe sees himself conducting research on human beings for which the traditional medical doctrine, to do no harm to human beings, is the first and foremost commandment. Dr. Kremer sees himself conducting research using "subhuman" humans, to whom that same commandment does not apply. In Dr. Kremer's case, this opens the floodgates to participating in horrendous evil. It includes doing evil willingly while, at the same time, believing that he is still acting well within a medical research mandate. Here evil is not recognized as a decisive issue. On the contrary, Kremer believed he was contributing to a noble cause while, at the same time, doing ground-breaking medical research.

We now turn to a person who fully realized that what he was doing was evil, who was aware of the difference between good and evil, and who nonetheless contributed to evil, and did it with zeal and imagination.

A NAZI BUREAUCRAT: CHIEF OF THE AUSCHWITZ EXTERMINATION CAMP

the same attitude of impersonal rationality is required to run successfully a large corporation, a death camp, a slave labor factory and an extermination center...[16]

the worst results of the events of 1930–33 [when Stalin's policies of destroying the Kulags and induced mass starvation produced approximately 14 million unnatural deaths in the Ukraine] was not so much the suffering of the peasantry, frightful though these were; it was the deep changes in the psychological outlook of those Communists who participated in this campaign and, instead of going mad, became professional bureaucrats for whom terror was henceforth a normal method of administration and obedience to any order from above [was] a high virtue...[17]

Modern management, in business and government, relies on routinizing the very large number of decisions that have to be made. Impersonality is its basic approach. Efficiency is its basic objective. The bureaucrat is its basic functionary.

Rudolf Hoess, the chief of the Auschwitz extermination camp, was such a bureaucrat. His career provides some striking lessons. Here was a modern bureaucrat, an administrative functionary, whose entire career was geared to administering evil. He "modernized" the management of evil in a manner that remains unsurpassed. In doing so he shows that virtually all dimensions of the bureaucrat's special approach to his work career lend themselves readily to the manufacture of evil. These dimensions include separating home life from work life, excluding personal feelings—emotions, friendships—from work activities, and striving for orderly, uninterrupted flow of work that rests on regularity and accountability.

Hoess's career demonstrates that components of ordinary daily living—the existence of packages, incremental decisions, riders and the use of personal autonomy—lend themselves to producing evil. For Hoess this meant carrying out an entire package of programs, even those elements he found repugnant; getting caught up in an evil course of action through a series of small, incremental decisions, which he knew to be evil and from which he saw no way to extricate himself; contributing honor by obeying authority under the rider of fostering German grandeur; and using his autonomy to make the murderous Auschwitz system work. For Hoess's subordinates, the guards at Auschwitz, there was autonomy to create an informal culture of their own. They used this autonomy to create a culture of cruelty, where cruelty was thoroughly enjoyable and rewarding, an end in itself.

Hoess did not personally kill people. He did not drop the lethal gas pellets into the gas chambers, just as Dr. Kremer did not personally inject the phenol that killed patients. He did little of the "dirty work." The torturing and killing of prisoners was left to underlings. Instead, Hoess was a specialist in modern bureaucratic administration, and he concerned himself mainly with organizational matters. This meant finding ways to organize the annihilation of vast numbers of people. Some days (and nights) the transports brought thousands upon thousands of prisoners to Auschwitz. On other days no transports arrived. To Hoess this situation required organizational flexibility, discipline, and ingenuity; and he provided them. He was effective and efficient in the mass production of death.

Hoess, the efficient bureaucrat, was also Hoess the bureaucratic careerist. Hoess was eager to please those bureaucrats in the Berlin headquarters who controlled his career. He knew that to accomplish the mission they had assigned to him required more than blind obedience. It required considerable ingenuity in the administration of an organization. And in practicing administrative ingenuity he became a master mass killer. He did this while serving as a functionary who operated entirely within and through the administration of a bureaucracy. Thereby this "ordinary little man" became an extraordinary agent of evil.[18]

Hoess's Life and Career: The Riders Take Root

Hoess was born in 1900, the son of an observant Catholic family. His father, a retired army colonel, wanted his son to be a priest. His upbringing was strict, and obedience to his parents was rigorously enforced.

During the First World War (1914–1918) Hoess volunteered to join the army. Hoess was then sixteen years old, and being a soldier held great attraction for him. In fact, to the end of his days he viewed himself as a soldier, an "ordinary foot soldier." After the war he joined a reactionary, rightist organization called the East Prussian Voluntary Corps. In 1922 he met Hitler and was greatly taken by him. He became one of Hitler's ardent followers and soon became embroiled in the Nazis' rough, harassing tactics. He apparently took part in a politically motivated murder in 1923. For this he served a six-year prison term, and his autobiography contains insightful ideas about the life of a prisoner.

Hoess strongly identified with the prisoners, as opposed to the authorities who run the prison. He had much to say about the brutality of guards—how they have it in their power to make life of the inmate utterly miserable or, instead, to make it somewhat bearable. Amazingly, at the time that Hoess wrote his autobiography, while he was again a prisoner, after *he* had been in charge of the most brutal of prisons, he still thought that he identified with those at the bottom: the guards and, to some extent, even with the prisoners.[19]

After his discharge from prison in 1929 Hoess married and took up farming. Farming, Hoess said, was a lifelong passion for him. As a child he had loved animals, trees, and solitary activities in rural places. Eventually Hoess had five children, two of them born while he was in concentration camp service.

In 1934, shortly after the Nazis gained control of the German government, Himmler, the SS chief, persuaded Hoess to join the SS. From then on Hoess became involved in the administration of concentration camps. He began as a guard at Dachau. There he served an "internship," learning his trade.

Hoess advanced in the SS hierarchy, but always in work relating to the administration of concentration camps. In 1940 he was assigned the task of establishing the camp at Auschwitz. Much of Hoess's autobiography is taken up with a review of the difficulties he encountered in establishing the camp: resources were limited; good staff members were hard to recruit; and the guidelines from Berlin headquarters were never precise enough, making it necessary to innovate a great deal. These are very typical bureaucratic complaints! They could have been made by the branch manager of a bank.

Eventually, Hoess was instructed to help devise the technology of mass murder on the grandest scale. He did so willingly and innovatively.

Hoess was often discouraged and frustrated. His autobiography frequently sounds as if nothing had gone very well. Yet his superiors must have been satisfied with his work, because they kept assigning him greater responsibilities. Hoess was a major contributor to transforming persecution and murder from an occasional outburst into a routine, mass-production process. Hoess, perhaps more than any other person, helped to create the *routinization* of evil in the concentration camps of Nazi Germany.

Hoess became the first chief of the Auschwitz camp, and except for a brief interim of service at the Berlin headquarters, he remained its chief. He was both the chief executive officer of Auschwitz throughout most of its existence and a major planner for achieving new missions whenever these were mandated by the Nazi government. The most notable of these was the mission of total extermination of the Jews.

Learning the Trade:
Becoming Immersed in a Package of Programs

The early Nazi concentration camps, such as Dachau, were geared to incarcerating a variety of prisoners, Jews and non-Jews. The prisoners were mistreated in the severest ways. Torture, up to and including murder, were commonplace, but the camps were not specifically extermination camps. Many prisoners were eventually released.[20]

Hoess learned the trade of concentration camp administrator at the Dachau and Sachsenhausen camps. At each camp he came under the influence of a severe taskmaster. At Dachau there was Theodore Eicke, the first commandant of a concentration camp, a man who personally inculcated into the SS the limitless brutality that was applied in all concentration camps. Hoess described him:

> [Eicke] deliberately whipped up...artificial hatred of the prisoners...to root out once and for all any sympathy they might feel [for the prisoners]...he succeeded in engendering in simple-natured men a hatred and antipathy for the prisoners which an outsider will find hard to imagine. This influence spread through all the SS men and the SS leaders who served in [the camps]...all the torture and ill-treatment inflicted upon the prisoners in the concentration camps can be explained by this "hate indoctrination"...[21]

Hoess believed that he, personally, was totally unsuited to serve in concentration camps.[22] He stated that he resented the brutality that took place. But he found it difficult to put an end to his involvement. He stated:

> this is where my guilt actually begins. It was clear to me that I was not suited to this sort of service, since in my heart I disagreed with [Commandant] Eicke's insistence that life in the concentration camp can be organized in this particular way. My sympathies lay too much with the prisoners, for I had myself lived their life too long and had personal experience of their needs.[23]

Hoess said he utterly disagreed with Eicke's attitude toward the inmates of the camps: "I disagreed with the way he whipped up the vilest emotions of hatred among the SS guards."

Hoess said he resented the brutality, but he became increasingly involved in carrying out brutality. Hoess said he could not extricate himself from the immediate situation in which he found himself because he did not have the courage to go to Himmler (his overall boss) and tell him that he was not suited for this work. And he had begun to enjoy wearing the SS uniform, and leaving his post in the concentration camp might lead to his being dismissed from the SS completely. He also had a sense of loyalty to Hitler and the Nazi system altogether. As Hoess saw it, all these factors were at work in the immediate situation in which he existed. In short, immediate, local circumstances made him decide to continue a course of action that contained components he regarded as distasteful.

Lamely, Hoess said, "by remaining in the concentration camps I accepted the ideas and the rules and regulations that there prevailed." Like many a careerist who thinks one is in the wrong occupation, Hoess said: "Silently I continue to hope that one day I might find another form of service." He sustained himself by what was perhaps the biggest self-deception of all: "I never grew indifferent to human suffering." He told himself: "who could have foreseen the horrifying tasks to be assigned [to the concentration camp] as the war went on?"[24]

Having reservations about, even revulsion for, some aspects of one's work does not necessarily keep one from engaging in these very aspects with utmost zeal. And Hoess did engage in evil with utmost zeal. Thus, the paradox that evil may be practiced by people who know better, is nowhere shown more explicitly than in the career of Hoess.

Hoess learned his trade through practice. On the first day after war was declared, Hoess, who was an officer by then, was put in charge of executing an SS colleague who had, by an act of carelessness, allowed a prisoner to escape. Hoess reported:

> I cannot understand to this day how I was able, quite calmly, to give the order [to the firing squad] to fire. I had been so busy with the preparations for the execution that it was not until it was over that I began to realize what had happened. All the officers who had been present at the shooting [of their colleague] assembled for a while in our mess. Oddly enough, no real conversation took place, and each of us just sat, wrapped in his own thoughts.... All of us were deeply affected by what had happened, not the least myself. This execution was always before my eyes to remind me of the demand that had been made upon us to exercise perpetual self-mastery and unbending severity.[25]

In short, this event became a *rider* to all of Hoess' subsequent activities as an SS officer.

After conducting his first execution, subsequent ones were easier. Execution of prisoners, in particular, became an almost daily occurrence, and they aroused none of the trauma of the first execution. Having survived the critical first increment, Hoess had learned his trade. He was immersed in it.

Obeying Authority—And Producing Honor

Hoess reported that his devout Catholic parents taught him the value of obedience to authority. "I had been taught since childhood to be absolutely obedient and meticulously tidy and clean." He reported that these traits were very useful to him while he was imprisoned (for murder) in the 1920s: "I did not find it difficult to conform to the strict discipline of prison. I conscientiously carried out all my duties. I completed the work allotted to me, and usually more...my cell was a model of neatness and cleanliness."

It is intriguing that Hoess prided himself not only on carrying out the work assigned to him by the authorities that imprisoned him, but also on doing even more than they demanded of him. He did not obey grudgingly. He obeyed enthusiastically. As a result, even though the orders came from a government he fought and hated he did not do the minimum of what he was asked to do. He did more than he was asked to do! He loved obedience to authority. He glorified obedience. Why?

Part of the answer is that Hoess was taught obedience by his parents and doubtless by the German schooling of his day. Obedience was drilled into him in his earliest years. If someone had asked him, What sort of person are you? He might well have answered, I am the sort of person who obeys orders. His conception of himself was, pridefully, that of a person who knew how to obey. Yet there was more to Hoess's obedience. Hoess sensed that by obeying authority he was *producing honor.*

Although we usually think that honor comes from the position one occupies (being a judge presumably carries more honor than being a garbage collector), honor is also attainable from how well one does one's job. Indeed, this is a way of producing honor. And this sort of honor is available to anyone, even to the holder of the lowliest positions, people who spend their lives obeying other people. For example, the traditional English butler occupies a lowly position—he is a servant—yet the typical (or stereotypical) English butler virtually oozes dignity and honor. He dresses in formal clothes (often handed down by his master), and he has the bearing and speech of a highly refined person. He serves as guardian of propriety and good manners for the upper classes, making sure that "good taste" prevails and that "unseemly" actions are prevented or quickly removed from view. Ironically, all this takes place even though the butler, himself, almost invariably coming from the lower classes, does not have the slightest chance of rising into the higher classes. He is disenfranchised from the classes whose way of life he so dedicatedly nurtures. His personal honor is kept alive by exuberant obedience. Thereby he contributes to his own honor. At the same time he contributes to the honor of the larger system, which he serves as underling and guardian of its public image.[26]

Hoess, too, sensed that he was contributing to his own honor and the honor of a larger system, even when he was obeying the detested government that was imprisoning him. He, personally, was making a contribution to a system of values that contained a major ideal: obey authority.

A fictionalized version of this phenomenon is described in the book *The Bridge on the River Kwai.*[27] The book portrays British soldiers who were interned in a Japanese prisoner-of-war camp during the Second World War. The prisoners thoroughly hated the Japanese authorities, and any collaboration with the Japanese was carried out with the greatest reluctance. When the Japanese ordered the prisoners to build a bridge over the River Kwai, a very difficult feat even for a trained construction team, the ranking British officer (who acted as chief of the prisoners) was placed in a quandary. He resented the Japanese as much as any of the men under him. Nonetheless, he decided to have the prisoners build the bridge. His decision was based on his desire to demonstrate the British tradition that a tough challenge can be met. He anticipated producing honor by giving the Japanese a taste of this British tradition and the strong British moral character it demonstrated. He believed that his obedience to a resented authority conferred *honor* upon those who did the obeying and upon the cultural tradition they represented. Thus obedience was regarded as an instrument for producing honor amid adverse circumstances.

More commonly, prisoners-of-war see themselves contributing to their own and their country's honor by occasional acts of *dis*-obedience to the authorities guarding them. Similarly, participants in Civil Rights movements, from Gandhi to Martin Luther King, Jr., used *dis*-obedience as a way of publicly demonstrating the honor of their cause. In a sense they were choosing to obey a higher moral authority rather than the then-existing social constraints of their society. They were using their autonomy to decide which authority is the most worthy of receiving obedience and, thereby, producing the greater amount of honor.

In Hoess's career, the most grotesque and most convoluted contribution to honor came after he assumed charge of Auschwitz. Himmler, acting on Hitler's instructions, had ordered the total extermination of the Jews. Hoess wrote in his diary that Himmler's order to him to develop a total extermination process, "certainly was an extraordinary and monstrous order," but it was completely unthinkable for Hoess to disobey. He obeyed with zeal. He devised the extermination procedures at Auschwitz, and he made sure they were carried out.

Why did Hoess obey orders he believed to be monstrous? Hoess knew that the SS permitted no disobedience to orders. But fear of punishment was not his reason for obeying this order. His obedience was based on nurturing honor, something far more subtle than fear of punishment.

Hoess knew, and accepted, Himmler's famous speech to SS officials on the Eastern Front (at Minsk, in August 1941), at a time when the mass killings had not yet been routinized in special camps. In that speech Himmler said the he was well aware that carrying out mass killings was horrible and that many persons felt terrible about it. (Some SS participants had committed suicide.) Himmler said SS soldiers should not blame themselves. Instead, they should take pride in themselves for having the fortitude and strength to go through with these horrible tasks. By doing so they were making a real contribution to the grand cause of Nazism.

Himmler did not paint a rosy picture. He acknowledged that involvement in mass killings, be it as an SS official or as an ordinary German soldier, was horrible. (Himmler is reported to have become nauseated when he viewed mass killings.) But, he said, there was a larger, nobler reality. There was that grand Nazi cause, Hitler's vision of a purified and awesomely great Germany, to whose realization these horrendous deeds made an essential contribution.

The individual who participated—who killed innocent men, women, and children—was creating honor by contributing to the realization of Hitler's vision of Germany. Indeed, it was precisely because the task was so difficult, so horrible, that one was making the greatest contribution to honor. After all, anyone can do easy tasks. Anyone can carry out pleasant orders. But carrying out horrible tasks really tests one's commitment to the grand cause. It demonstrates one's fortitude. In Himmler's words, whether one was "truly hard" was put to the test when one had to go through with horrible assignments.

Hoess believed this. The killings at Auschwitz took place under his command. He thought they were really horrible, and he reported scenes that he regarded as grisly, being carried out in *his* camp, under *his* orders. For example, a Jewish man, under temporary reprieve from death and working as a member of the Sonderkommando unit, had the task of dragging corpses out of the gas chambers. One day Hoess saw him stop for a moment. Why did he stop? The man had just noticed that the corpse he was dragging was that of his wife. Hoess was horrified. (Just as his SS men frequently, but privately, expressed horror to him.) But, Hoess believed, the program had to go on. There was honor in obedience. On the road to obedience one could permit no questioning of the orders. It would break the cycle of honor through unflinching obedience. Hence, Hoess made great efforts to ensure absolute obedience. He, himself, had to set an example. He said:

> There was no doubt in the mind of any of us that Hitler's order had to be obeyed regardless, and that it was the duty of the SS to carry it out. Nevertheless, we were all touched by severe doubts.
>
> I myself dared not admit such doubt. In order to make my subordinates carry on with their task, it was psychologically essential that I myself appear convinced of the necessity for this gruesomely harsh order. Everyone watched me.... I had to exercise self-control in order to prevent my innermost doubts and feelings of oppression from becoming apparent.
>
> I had to appear cold and indifferent to events that must have wrung the heart of anyone possessed of human feeling. I might not even look away when afraid lest my emotions got the upper hand. I had to watch coldly, while mothers with laughing or crying children went into the gas chambers.... I had to see everything. I had to watch hour after hour...the removal and burning of the bodies...the whole grisly, interminable business. I had to stand for hours on end in the ghastly stench, while the mass graves were being opened and the bodies dragged out and burned.... I had to do all this because I was the one to whom everyone looked, because I had to show them all that I did not merely issue orders, and make the regulations but was also prepared to be present at whatever task I had assigned to my subordinates.[28]

On another occasion, he said: "I [was] aware of the impending horror, namely the Extermination Order [to kill the Gypsies].... Nothing surely is harder than to grit one's teeth and go through with such a thing, coldly, pitilessly, and without mercy."[29]

Hoess believed that acting "coldly, pitilessly, and without mercy" became an essential part of his obedience to authority. Hoess had learned the importance of what he called *inflexible harshness* from his SS teacher while he underwent training at Dachau. Then, at Auschwitz, this orientation became a guiding rider to the package of behavior comprising his daily life. It helped him believe that by obeying horrible orders he was making a valuable contribution to the honor of the Nazi cause and to his own honor and sense of self-worth as a member of the SS.

Living with Evil:
Using One's Autonomy to Create Distinctive Packages

When one reads Hoess's autobiography one is struck by the fact that he wrote so sensitively. He claimed to be a man of tender feelings. He said he abhorred violence and suffering, and perhaps he really meant it. Yet, how could he live with himself? After all, he did design and implement the most monstrous actions that humans can conceive.

This is a great incongruity, the sensitive man doing monstrous things. To preserve our own sanity and reduce the cognitive dissonance in the way we look at the world, we must find a way to reconcile this incongruity. We could start by denying one of the statements. Namely, we can entertain the idea that Hoess was not the sensitive man he portrays himself to be. He was trying to deceive. He was lying—to himself and to everyone else.

The possibility that Hoess was lying is attractive. Most of us would prefer to believe that a man like Hoess was lying when he claims to be sensitive to human suffering. We would assert that Hoess was not only *not* a sensitive human being but, on the contrary, he was among the coldest, the most vicious, and most evil of members of the human species. He was a monster in human disguise.

This is a very plausible answer. It asserts our rightly felt anger at the man and his deeds. It is the easiest answer, requiring little subtlety. But it is a very unsatisfactory answer. In fact, it does not explain anything. To say that a person who does monstrous things is a monster, explains nothing. It merely puts a label on the person. If we want to confront a real challenge to the mind we will face up to the possibility that Hoess did monstrous things, and did them with passion and zeal, yet he was sensitive to the monstrosity of his deeds. This is not easy, especially if we do not want to write off Hoess as pathological, as a demented individual, but instead see him as a person operating from within the range of ordinary human behavior.

At the very least, Hoess was an extreme version of Dr. Doe,

who disliked some aspects of his work, but went on doing the disliked aspects and did them diligently and thoroughly. At the very least, also, he was a person who lived for honor. And in the pursuit of honor he adapted to the very grotesque *context* in which he found himself. The immediate context, itself, played a vital part in making his evil possible, and so did his own contribution to that context.

Of course the social context—the pressures emanating from the Nazi hierarchy under which Hoess operated—was *not* accountable for Hoess's personal behavior in response to that context. No one can claim that poor, sensitive Rudolf Hoess was coerced into the brutality he practiced at Auschwitz, that he was merely "the product" of his social environment. He was certainly influenced by the constraints placed on him by the Nazi context. But he was surely responsible for his own initiatives in response to that context, using his considerable autonomy. That response included helping to *invent* the system in which massive evil took place. And Hoess, more than anyone else, made that system work! He did so by creating for himself a distinctive behavioral package for a happy and separate family life, despite its proximity to the camp; and he did so by creating a distinctive behavioral package for administering Auschwitz.

A Happy Family Life: Separating Home from Work   Hoess lived with his wife and children in a house near the Auschwitz extermination camp. To a remarkable extent he was able to live a quiet family life. His life resembled that of an Army officer living with his wife and children near an Army base, as it was typically lived before the modern woman's movement. (In such an Army context children see their father go off to work in the morning—to train to kill—and return home to them and their mother in the evening, to play with them, to ask about their homework, to fix things around the house, to go to bed with their home-bound mother at night.)

The Hoess house was located in its own grounds. Mrs. Hoess set the tone for gracious family dinners and kindly surveillance of the children. The atmosphere was civilized. There were servants—camp inmates—who took care of the cooking and much of the menial work. The children had room to play. There was time for family togetherness, for quiet play on the bucolic grounds, for walks in the woods. There was no scarcity of food. There was no need to skimp and save. Much of the economic harshness of life in wartime Germany was absent. Hoess wrote that his wife believed their family life was a bit of a paradise, and he obviously shared this belief.

To achieve this bit of paradise Hoess rigidly separated home from work. He would not permit life in the camp to intrude into his family routines. At home there was no talk about camp brutalities, about the fate of this or that individual Jew. The servants knew very well that their personal suffering had better be hidden from the Hoesses. Mrs. Hoess was kind to the servants, but they knew there were limits to what they could tell her.

Hoess himself occasionally came home feeling troubled about events at the camp. He made it a point not to talk about these feelings to his wife. He did not want his family involved. Instead, he would go for a walk by himself. Or he would go for a ride on one of his beloved horses. After a while he became calm. Then he would return home.

Hoess created a family life that was relatively separate from his work. It was a life of simple joys, of nurturent family interactions. Although the chimneys of the camp were visible from his house, they might as well have been a hundred miles away. Family life was a context of its own. It was warm. It was rewarding. It was comfortable German burgherhood.

Creating the Context for Evil: Separating Home from Hell Is a Mental Accomplishment   Hoess's family life took place in the context of his home. Hoess's Auschwitz life took place in the context of the camp. Each life contained a reality of its own: an outlook and a posture to the world, a set of duties and activities, as well as rewards and satisfactions. Furthermore, from the vantage point of each reality, the content of the other was virtually unthinkable. On the one hand, in the Hoess household life itself had some measure of sanctity and grace. On the other hand, in the Auschwitz camp life was held in utter contempt. It was treated as an easily expendable commodity.

If the two contexts were separated by a few centuries or by a geographic distance of several thousand miles, one might almost be able to comprehend the coexistence of such different worlds, one bestial and vile, the other nurturant and humane. Yet there was no such separation. Both existed at the same time, in full physical view of each other. What is more, the major actor in both contexts was the same person.

Obviously, the physical separation of the two contexts is not the real issue. The real issue is Hoess's mental separation of the two contexts. We are talking about a *mental construction* of reality; and mental constructions are real, especially in the way they influence human behavior. In our daily life we continually bring mental constructions to bear on our situation. Through mental constructions we organize the reality in which we live.

In Hoess's case, he took care that the camp and his house were separate, but physical separation played a minor part. The basic separation took place in his mind, and in his wife's mind. It was the Hoesses' mental construction of reality that enabled the two worlds to coexist as separate entities.

Obviously, then, what is extraordinary about Hoess is not that he used mental constructions to help create the world in which he lived, but the degree of his success. He was able to separate two grotesquely disparate worlds that were actually intertwined. He was able to nurture each of them while keeping them from intruding into one another. This was a considerable mental accomplishment. What made it possible?

The answer lies in how Hoess used his *autonomy* to create a distinctive behavioral package to serve as guidelines for his family life. Although Hoess operated under orders from the SS leadership, he still had considerable autonomy to create that package. In his ongoing daily behavior he continually delineated and reinforced the content of the package. He made choices. He fostered activities of which he approved, and he crushed activities of which he disapproved.

A major element of Hoess's separate family package was that he deliberately created barriers between the camp and his home. He was innovative when it came to erecting psychological and communications barriers between the two realms. He was innovative, for example, when he deliberately decided to go for a walk or on a horseback ride when he knew that his feelings, based on recent camp events, might spill over into his family life.

Because SS instructions did not specify what Hoess would do every minute of the day, they left him enough autonomy so that he could be innovative in how he worked out the relations between the camp and his family life. He used this autonomy to devise very effective ways of separating the two.

Hoess's wife contributed. She built an active family life, with its own rituals, its family celebrations, its daily routines that nurtured a sense of family well-being. Hoess, himself, supported all this by his quiet approval. Given the German authoritarian family structure, he could have snuffed out all nurturent family life had he wished to do so. Instead he used his autonomy to foster a course of action that created a mighty separation between his family and the camp. Toward this objective he made it abundantly clear that there were limits to the indulgence and intimacy that his family would show to camp inmates who worked in his home. This was one of many ways in which he fostered separation between his family and the camp.

In summary, the techniques Hoess used to create his mental separation of his home from the concentration camp were very successful because Hoess had considerable power to assert his will and considerable autonomy to create and perpetuate a distinctive behavior package for a separate family life. He used both. In particular, he used his autonomy to be flexible in coping with stresses and strains and to devise techniques that ensured relative insulation of the two contexts from one another.

Creating the Context for Evil: Packaging a New World   In addition to separating his Auschwitz world from his home surroundings, Hoess also *packaged* the Auschwitz world into a distinctive psychological entity for its administrative staff.

Packaging means bringing together very different items of behavior and linking them. Because the different components are linked the individual perceives the package as a single entity. It then becomes virtually impossible for that individual to separate the component parts. If one dislikes one of the components and wants to reject it, one is faced with having to reject the total package. This is often difficult, particularly when one of the components is very attractive and one does not wish to abandon it.

For example, advertising for cigarettes often links smoking with active outdoor living, successful sex, and friendly get-togethers of congenial people. Many people accept this package, and smoke cigarettes, because the package includes a number of different ingredients, any one of which may be especially appealing.

One of the actual components of the smoking package, the poisonous character of cigarettes, is overshadowed by the advertised components of the package.

Thus packaging is an artful application of psychology. In this sense Hoess was a practicing psychologist. At Auschwitz he molded the staff of the camp by packaging the evil activities. Furthermore, for Hoess there were two packages: the package he presented to his staff and his personal package. Hoess's Auschwitz staff package contained (1) the Nazi ideological justification for the program of extermination, (2) adherence to some forms of traditional "morality," and (3) perhaps most important, a government-operated bureaucracy, where work had much of the rhythm, tempo, pressures, and rewards found in every bureaucracy. Hoess's personal package was based on his own life history. Together, these two packages constituted a tightly organized way of conducting a murderous course of action and personally coming to terms with living with evil. Let me illustrate how it actually worked, beginning with the staff package:

Hoess's subordinate officers occasionally expressed doubts about their mission. They did so when they talked to Hoess privately. Hoess invariably assured them that it was utterly essential to believe in the Nazi theme that Jews had to be exterminated, that Jews represented a mortal threat to Germany. This *ideological justification*, Hoess claimed, was crucial. He gave it deliberately, as a tactic, to safeguard the Auschwitz package. He himself shared the misgivings of his subordinate officers, but he expressed them only to some of his own SS colleagues *outside* Auschwitz— where the misgivings were not apt to break apart the package that constituted the psychological structure of Auschwitz.[30] For Hoess and his colleagues the ideological justification for their deeds meant that the ongoing actions at Auschwitz were not of purely local relevance. On the contrary, they saw their actions as part of a great plan that fit into an ideological scheme of national goals. The activities at Auschwitz "made sense" to Hoess and his staff because they helped implement nationally approved goals—the government said so. Their actions were not illegal or deviant.

Hoess claimed to link Auschwitz to a semblance of traditional *morality*. Amid what he admitted to be a life of horrors, he claimed to enforce a large measure of traditional social morality—taking steps against stealing, against guards' taking sexual advantage of prisoners, against "undue" brutality. He claimed to be appalled by female Capos' turning into virtual beasts, "tearing [Jewish] women to pieces, killing them with axes and throttling them—it was simply gruesome." He made serious efforts, he claimed, to stop such abuses and to get a better class of personnel. But, alas, it was difficult!

From his own days as a prisoner Hoess remembered guards who were "malicious, evil-minded, basically bad, brutal, inferior, common creatures…they [did] not know the meaning of pity or kind warm fellow feeling. They seize[d] every opportunity to terrorize prisoners…" He wanted none of this at Auschwitz!

Hoess brought a *work ethic* to Auschwitz. Above the entrance gate he erected the sign "Arbeit macht frei" (work makes one free). "All my life I have thoroughly enjoyed working. I myself derive no real satisfaction from my labors unless I have completed a good job of work thoroughly…"

Linked to work, Hoess loved *modern technology*. He was pleased that Auschwitz used modern gas chamber technology. It "minimized suffering," for the guards and the victims—a link with traditional humane concerns. He was well aware that, before the advent of this mass murder technology, there had been mass killings by shooting, particularly behind the front lines as the German armies advanced into Russia and Poland. "Many gruesome scenes are said to have taken place…. Many members of the Einsatzkommandos, unable to endure wading through blood any longer, had committed suicide. Some had even gone mad." Through the gas chamber technology "I was…relieved to think that we are spared all those blood baths and the victims would also be spared suffering until their last moment came." Packaged in mass production technology, the killings at Auschwitz were preferable to those elsewhere!

Few sane people are likely to agree with Hoess's kindly view of Auschwitz—that he minimized suffering, that he was concerned for the feelings of the victims and the guards, and that under the circumstances he did the most humane things he could do. Yet one must admit that by including a "morality" and a "work ethic," however twisted, Hoess created a package that linked up with traditional German values and thereby added credibility and coherence to the package that helped to hold it together.

From the vantage point of the victims, Auschwitz was a

world of sustained horror—of constant cruelty, suffering, mortal danger, and great unpredictability. It was an organized system of hell. For Hoess and his colleagues, on the other hand, the Auschwitz package was very different. Auschwitz was a way of life in the confines of a bureaucracy.

In his autobiography Hoess repeatedly mentioned the bureaucratic features of life at Auschwitz. It was a life of schedules, work routines, meeting deadlines, remaining in good standing with the headquarters in Berlin. It was a life of personal careers. One's career, at any one time, was linked up with one's work in one particular organization. One's performance in that organization was subject to scrutiny. One who performed poorly, who upset one's superiors in Berlin, could rapidly end up in an infantry unit on the Eastern Front, where life expectancy was notoriously short. For gross errors one could be shot or quickly transformed from an overseer of gas chambers to a victim of gas chambers. This threat was made openly and frequently. It was one of the bureaucratic facts of life that one's career hinged on one's job performance. This was as real to Hoess and his staff as the lethal horrors were real to the inmates.

Another dimension of the Auschwitz bureaucracy was that it created a separate and distinct *culture of cruelty*. This culture went far beyond the officially specified cruelties. It developed a system of social relationships where cruelty was a basis for one's personal reputation and social standing. This was so fundamental that it deserves a separate discussion. I shall do so in the next section.

Hoess's personal package, the one he used to justify his part in mass murder to himself, evolved during the course of his life. As he saw it, the evils of Nazism were imprinted during his early years as a concentration camp guard. Under the tutelage of Eicke, the commandant of Dachau, he discovered the limitless brutality of the camps. He resented that brutality, but the brutality was packaged in a way that made Hoess continue to adhere to it—to *all* of it, even the part he resented. Hoess reported that his personal concentration camp package included the following items: his fondness for the SS uniform, his fear of being fired, his loyalty to Hitler, his loyalty to the Nazi party and its program, including the "need to eradicate asocials and criminals," his lack of the courage needed to request release from concentration camp assignments, his fear that he would become a laughing stock if he requested a different assignment, and, as his career advanced, especially after he became head of Auschwitz, the fact that he had more and more to lose. It became increasingly difficult to reject the package. Hoess's personal package remained with him throughout his career in the SS. It constituted the background to his promotion of evil at Auschwitz. It provided him with a framework for his daily activities at Auschwitz.

Creating Evil the Bureaucratic Way

Every bureaucratic organization, be it a factory, a hospital, a prison, a government "bureau," or a concentration camp, can have two components. One component is *a system of control*, which coexists with the other component, *a system of autonomy*. Traditional descriptions of bureaucracies concentrated on the controls. The most famous of these was contributed by Max Weber, a sociologist who lived at the turn of the century. He gave detailed descriptions of the system of control one finds in government bureaucracies, such as departments one would find within the federal government. In such a system of control there are explicit rules for guiding the behavior of the bureaucracy's officials in response to problems that might arise; the career of officials is geared to carrying out these rules; success in a bureaucratic career depends on how well the bureaucrat performs tasks, as judged by those higher in the bureaucratic hierarchy; there is clear separation between the official's work and personal life; and, within the bureaucratic organization, there are clearly defined objectives for the organization and clearly stipulated steps for reaching the objectives. In short, there is a system of control geared to efficient administration. It uses human beings (and machines) to maximize efficiency.

Hannah Arendt[31] gave a description of the system of control and the system of autonomy that coexisted at Auschwitz:

> one must always keep in mind that Auschwitz had been established for *administrative* massacres that were to be executed according to the strictest rules and regulations. These rules and regulations had been laid down by the desk murderers, and they seemed to exclude—probably they were meant to exclude—all individual initiative either for better or worse. The extermination of millions was planned to function like a machine: the

arrivals from all over Europe; the selections on the ramp, and the subsequent selections among those who had been able-bodied on arrival; the division into categories (all old people, children, and mothers with children were to be gassed immediately); the human experiments; the system of "trustee prisoners," the capos, and the prisoner-commandos, who manned the extermination facilities and held privileged positions. Everything seemed foreseen and hence predictable—day after day, month after month, year after year. And yet, what came out of the bureaucratic calculations was the exact opposite of predictability. It was complete arbitrariness. In the words of Dr. Wolken—a former inmate, now a physician in Vienna...

"*Everything changed from day to day*. It depended on the officer in charge, on the roll-call leader, on the block leader, on their moods"—most of all, it turns out, on their moods. "Things could happen one day that were completely out of the question two days later.... One and the same work detail could be either a death detail...or it could be a fairly pleasant affair." Thus, one day the medical officer was in a cheerful mood and had the idea of establishing a block for convalescents; two months later, all the convalescents were rounded up and sent into the gas. What the desk murderers had overlooked...was the human factor.[32]

What Arendt found at Auschwitz is very typical for bureaucracies. In every modern bureaucratic organization the participants have their tasks spelled out for them in official rules and regulations that specify what the individual is expected to accomplish while participating in the mission of the organization. But toward the middle of her statement Arendt mentioned that there was activity at Auschwitz that deviated from the official controls. Much of the life at Auschwitz seemed to be entirely arbitrary and capricious. She ascribed this to the "human factor." What she caught a glimpse of was a system of autonomy that can exist within bureaucracies. Such systems of autonomy derive from the fact that the bureaucracy's rules and regulations usually leave a great deal of room for interpretation by the individual who makes decisions during day-to-day work activities. The result is some autonomous behavior at all levels, from the top executive to the lowliest functionary, from concentration camp commander down to the individual camp guard.

The potential for autonomy among an organization's personnel can lead to distinctly structured subcultures within these organizations. In the social sciences the best known of these subcultures are the informal cultures of blue-collar factory workers. The characteristics of informal cultures in factories are important because it turns out that Auschwitz guards had an informal culture as well. It contained some striking similarities to the informal cultures found among workers in traditional American factories (before the Japanese-inspired changes).

Some Lessons Learned from Factories Sociologists long ago observed and described (especially in the 1930s and 1940s) how assembly-line workers augment the tedium of their work by creating entire systems of behavior with which to fill the working day. Typically, there is informal banter among a group of assembly-line workers. At first such banter seems random or haphazard. Yet, when one listens carefully one discovers that the banter is not random at all. It has distinct patterns. For one thing, there is *specialization*: "Joe" is always the butt of jokes and is never shown respect; "Harry" is respected for his seriousness; "Bill" is a storyteller; "Janet" is an attentive listener; "Mary" is a constant debunker, of anything and everything; and "Harriet" is an uncritical believer—no matter how outrageous a tale Bill tells, Harriet believes every word of it. Everyone within the group knows everyone else's role, and that, too, is part of the sport of daily conversation. In short, a group often develops a culture of its own—a culture that may include a lively and rich social process. Life is made interesting by inventive games and by specialization. Harry does not suddenly become a prankster. If he did, he would undermine his standing in the group. Janet does not suddenly become a debunker. If she did, she would undermine her standing in the group. Harriet does not suddenly ask searching questions. If she did, she would undermine her standing in the group.

For the group, much of the flavor of daily life comes from the inventiveness of the participants. And yet the inventiveness is balanced by predictability. One never knows which tall tale Bill will tell next, but it is safe to say that every few days he will produce one. One does not know just how Mary will debunk Bill's next story, but it is certain that she will find an imaginative way of debunking it. Each has a *reputation* for a specialized way of participating.

In short, this subculture—this culture within the larger culture of the factory—has a way of organizing the autonomy of its members. On the one hand, there is creativity: each individual operates autonomously in his or her particular zone, within which innovation and the use of imagination are encouraged. On the other hand, although creativity emerges in the specialized zones, there are clear boundaries to the practice of autonomy.

This is a way of encouraging the exercise of autonomy while channeling it. Autonomy—in the form of innovative, imaginative behavior—is thereby stabilized. The rhythm of daily living combines autonomy and control.

Sometimes the worker subculture is used to control productivity, to intimidate rate busters. Early sociological studies concentrated on these aspects. These studies showed that autonomous behavior includes harsh behavior, which can be rudiments for real evil. For instance, the worker who works too hard, who goes beyond the production quota that the group has informally established, is soon teased about his or her rate busting. If this does not bring one's production down, one may find one's lunch box stolen, one's work sabotaged and eventually one's work life made thoroughly unpleasant. The attacks on this worker increase incrementally, becoming ever-more cruel, under the overall rider that this worker is out-of-step with the group's norms and therefore deserves to be punished.

More recently, it has become clear that worker subcultures can be used to get work done more efficiently (in quality control circle patterns popularized in Japan); they help the factory to achieve its mission. In both aspects, the autonomous subculture has content that bears on the mission of the whole organization. In both aspects, too, the autonomous subculture augments the formal rules of the factory. Thus autonomy is not random "freedom" to do whatever participants wish to do. In the traditional American factory, for example, the assembly-line worker can spend much of the day talking about his or her outside concerns—the young men and women may spend hours recounting, and partially reenacting, courting adventures; older men and women may talk about illness and problems of middle age in unending jokes about loss of virility and gaining and losing riches. Neither group will spend time talking about, let alone making decisions about, pricing or product policies, areas in which they have no autonomy at all.

The traditional factory executive, on the other hand, can indeed spend work time using his or her autonomy on policy making. But he (usually it has been a man) does not have the autonomy to spend work hours telling colleagues about his courtship adventures, particularly if they do not directly appear to augment his factory duties. Each participant, blue-collar worker or executive, has autonomy only in certain zones and not in others.

In summary, informal cultures in factories exhibit three notable behavior characteristics among the participants:

- *Autonomy:* the participants carry out some independent, uncontrolled, and often innovative activities.

- *Specialization:* each participant has autonomy in a particular zone, whose boundaries are known; and based on how the individual uses that autonomy, that individual develops a *reputation.*

- *Content:* there is a distinctive content to the ongoing behavior. The content usually relates to the participants' life inside and outside the factory. Often, in a playful manner, they address issues that are of real importance to themselves. Hence, the content of the banter among young men and women is likely to be around sex and dating; that of middle-aged men is likely to be around yearning for economic security and better health; that of middle-aged women is likely to be around family management matters. All of them may dwell on stabilizing productivity.

The contribution of informal cultures to life in factories is that they provide workers with a measure of sociability and conviviality, with relief from boredom and a chance for each person to express some individuality, even creativity—in a setting where the daily work is entirely stupefying. In short, they are basically wholesome and benign social processes. But, as the crackdown on rate busters shows, they also contain something very different: rudiments of cruelty. Ordinarily the cruelty is kept in check. At Auschwitz cruelty was not kept in check. There cruelty became the core content of a distinctive informal culture—where cruelty went beyond even the officially mandated murderous cruelty.

The Culture of Cruelty at Auschwitz   *The mission of Auschwitz was the systematic extermination of innocent people. To accomplish this mission there were official, formal procedures for carry-*

*ing out massacres. Yet in addition to these official, formal proce-
dures there emerged other forms of massacre. These were produced
by the Auschwitz personnel who, using their own autonomy, informally developed a distinctive culture of cruelty that augmented the
officially prescribed patterns of cruelty. In this culture of cruelty
behavior evolved where new forms of cruelty were invented,
refined, and repeatedly reenacted; where evil was deliberately
courted, with full knowledge that it was evil; where a guard's personal reputation, one's status as an Auschwitz guard, was based on
innovative contributions to cruelty.*

The behavior of Auschwitz guards I am about to discuss is
based on the information brought out at the trial of several of them,
held in Frankfurt in 1965.[33] Their behavior included deliberately
specializing, as well as using their autonomy to establish a reputation with a distinctive content; namely, the cultivation of cruelty.

Among the Auschwitz guards *specialization* was practiced
very explicitly.

For example, Wilhelm Boger loved torture. He invented the
"Boger swing," an instrument of torture of which the Spanish
Inquisition might have been proud.[34]

Stefan Boretzki was a specialist at killing prisoners with one
blow of the edge of the hand.[35] When he was not outrightly
killing he "had a habit of hitting people in the face and breaking
their noses."[36]

Gerhard Palitzsch specialized in devising games for shooting
prisoners. "In the camp we called him William Tell."[37]

Oswald Kaduk also was fond of shooting prisoners, but he did
not invent games, as Palitzsch did. He was merely prepared to shoot
prisoners at any moment. "He was always ready to shoot. Kaduk
was known to be more trigger-happy than any other SS man."[38]

Joseph Klehr was a medical orderly who specialized in killing
people by injecting phenol into their hearts. He killed thousands,
perhaps as many as 20,000.[39] When doctors did not send him victims fast enough, he went to the camp's sick wards and picked up
more people. Strictly speaking, this was against the rules, but
when it came to murder there was room for zeal, using one's
autonomy to improvise.

Emil Bednarek specialized in the routine of putting prisoners
in cold showers, then sending them out into the cold, then beat-

ing them, then sending them back to the shower. He continued this sequence until death mercifully intervened.

In short, the SS men were not undifferentiated functionaries. They were modern people: they were specialists.

An individual's specialization produced a *reputation*. That reputation was not left to chance. Instead, one's reputation was usually nurtured deliberately, often through advertising of one's particular specialty in cruelty.

Specific routines, such as Bednarek's, were well known. Bednarek was also known to trample prisoners to death and, then, feeling in the proper mood, to go to his room to pray, presumably to thank God for giving him such fulfillment.

Boger's swing was known too. Boger frequently bragged about it. And known, as well, was Boger's trampling on small children and smashing their heads against a wall.[40] A surviving inmate described him: "Boger was the devil of the camp. He was always riding around on his bicycle. The prisoners called him 'death on wheels'."[41] Sometimes, while riding on his bicycle, Boger dragged a prisoner behind him. A surviving Russian prisoner said: "We called [Boger] the howling death."[42]

A former pharmacist, Dr. Capesius, told prisoners: "In me you will get to know the devil."[43]

Of Percy Broad it was said that he was "death in kid gloves."[44] "It was generally known...that Broad was very dangerous for the camp inmates."[45]

Kaduk had a reputation as a man of zeal. A survivor said: "Kaduk was considered the camp scourge by the prisoners. Kaduk became more than just another SS man—a symbol.... He was present at all executions [presumably by his own choice]. Kaduk was the man who was always first."[46] It was known that with the help of a Capo, Kaduk pushed the head of a prisoner into a tub of water until the prisoner drowned.

In short, many SS officers had their own individualized reputation for cruelty. Each had a mark of distinction earned through his own effort and achievement in cruelty. These officers did not merely carry out the duties and assignments given them. They did more—they innovated. And they devoted considerable effort to making sure that their innovations, their specialized contributions to cruelty, were widely known.

All this was facilitated by the fact that an SS guard's duties allowed a great deal of flexibility. The individual SS officer had room to interpret instructions. Here he had *autonomy*. By making use of that autonomy he could create his own personalized reputation for cruelty.

In the culture of cruelty at Auschwitz, cruel deeds were crucial to an officer's "economic" standing. Auschwitz was a social economy in which the officer's credit rating depended on cruel deeds. The more grotesquely cruel the deeds, the higher the officer's standing in that economy. Conversely, mercy to prisoners quickly cost an officer his standing. For instance, protecting a prisoner against cruelty could abruptly lead to the officer being declared bankrupt in the system—and sharing the prisoner's fate or, short of that, being sent to the Eastern Front. This "economic" system of accounting was enforced most blatantly for the Capos, the inmates who worked for the SS as handlers of bodies after gassing, or as supervisors of living fellow-inmates. Theirs was a very marginal existence in that economy. Any deviation from cruelty would immediately lead to death for the "deviant" Capo.

An SS officer's reputation for cruelty was not an awkward personal quirk. It was part of the officer's membership in the informal culture of cruelty of Auschwitz. This culture included actively evaluating the ongoing performance of its members.

In this system the SS officer's cruel deeds were performed publicly, where they could be seen and noted by his colleagues and by the inmates. By contrast, a "good" deed—an occasional act of kindness and concern for an inmate—had to be performed furtively, in private. There must be no witnesses who were in a position to record and charge the officer's performance against his standing in the culture of cruelty.

Interestingly, the same SS officer who epitomized cruelty in his public acts could, occasionally, be kind in private. Arendt reported, in her introduction to the book on the trials of SS guards held in 1965, "there was 'almost no SS man who could not claim to have saved someone's life'...and most of the survivors...owed their lives to these 'saviors'..."[47]

For example, I can cite an act of kindness by an SS officer toward my brother Ludwig. It occurred shortly before the Second World War, while my brother was briefly incarcerated in a Nazi prison. One evening the SS officer who beat the prisoners the most cruelly asked my brother to come to his room. There he gave my brother food—an extra herring. Given the starvation-level diet the prisoners were getting, this was a substantial gift. To my knowledge, this gift came without strings attached—my brother was not asked to become a spy for the SS.

Such examples suggest that SS officers could still distinguish good from evil. But one should not assume that, for this reason, they did evil deeds halfheartedly, or against their will. In fact, good and evil were sometimes deliberately juxtaposed to underscore a clear preference for evil. Evil was flaunted:

A woman was sent chocolates and flowers after she gave birth to a child; the following day these same benefactors sent her to the gas chambers.[48]

One of the most ghoulish SS officers would, on occasion, "distribute sausages to children" and, then, continue his ghoulish deeds.[49]

One "medical officer who handed tens of thousands over to death could also save a woman who had reminded him of his youth" and, then, continue unperturbedly sending innocents to their death.[50]

Klehr specialized in killing prisoners by injecting them with phenol while another prisoner assisted him by holding the victim. One day the assistant cried while assisting Klehr. The next day Klehr asked him why he had cried. The assistant answered that he cried because he was assisting Klehr in killing his own father. Klehr then jovially said: "Why didn't you tell me? I would have spared him!" (My guess is that the likelihood of Klehr's sparing the man's father was somewhere between nil and zero; that Klehr's statement was deliberately sadistic, to make the hapless man feel that he was really responsible for his own father's death.)

Individual guards boasted of their brutality. One of them said: "other guards [have] been exceptionally brutal, but they could not hold a candle to me."[51] Much of the boasting was geared to showing that the boaster was aware of just how extraordinarily evil his deeds were.

A survivor reported:

I saw (Oberscharfuehrer [Otto] Moll) take a child from its mother, carry it over to Crematory IV, which had two pits [where human bodies were being burned] and throw the child into the seething [human] fat. Then he went up to his "servant," a former French featherweight boxing champion, and said to him: "It is possible to have one's fill."[52]

Another survivor, a woman who worked in an SS office, reported: "Once [SS man] Broad came back...we were already at work. His uniform had blood stains. He came with [Gerhard] Lachmann and said: 'You know, Gerhard, it spurted like from an animal.' Then he handed me the coat and I went to clean it."[53]

Finally, another witness recalled:

> one particular day in November, 1944...Jewish children were brought to Auschwitz. A truck came and stopped for a moment.... A little boy jumped off. He held an apple in his hand. [SS men] Boger and Drasner were standing in the doorway. I was standing at the window. The child was standing next to the car with the apple and was enjoying himself. Suddenly Boger went over to the boy, grabbed his legs, and smashed his head against the wall. Then he calmly picked up the apple. And Drasner told me to wipe "that" off the wall. About an hour later I was called to Boger to interpret in an interrogation and saw him eating the child's apple.[54]

This deed has a theatrical quality. Boger gruesomely killed an innocent child for an apple. He later ate the apple in front of a witness to the murderous deed. It was no accident that Boger ate the apple when the witness was there to see it. He was *flaunting* his evil. He was issuing a trumpeted announcement that life was cheap, that he knew of the child's innocence and was prepared to trample upon that innocence. His act was a combination of cruelty and calculated advertising of his commitment to evil.

Boger was not the only SS officer capable of this combination. Other SS officers murdered babies in front of their mothers, thereby advertising their crime to the person who is most deeply hurt by it. As targeted advertising, this assuredly reached the audience that would most fully understand the message: the officer's commitment to unbridled evil. It was not enough to do evil. Boger, and the others, wanted an appropriate reputation for evil.

In terms of personal reputation for evil, one of the most flamboyant Auschwitz officers was Dr. Joseph Mengele. He was a stylized killer—a man with a reputation for a distinctive way of packaging brutality, by combining it with considerable elegance in his personal appearance and charm in his manners. His specialty centered on the way he participated in the "selection" process, deciding who would live and who would die, doing so with a distinctive flair. He was also known for conducting experiments on twins, which were carried out with "murderous scientific fanaticism."[55] He combined passionate interest in disease with utter disregard for human life. When Mengele noticed the slightest biological abnormality in an inmate's appearance, he would have that person killed, then carry out a detailed autopsy, and announce the results shortly thereafter. Here, too, it was not enough to do evil. By announcing the results of the autopsy to his colleagues he was advertising his deeds. He was maintaining his chosen reputation.

Cruelty became the distinctive *content* of the informal culture among Auschwitz guards. A premium was placed on creating cruelty and treating it as a form of creative art. Each Auschwitz SS officer filled an assigned position. But within that position many devised their own way of practicing cruelty creatively.

Each SS officer's specialized piece of creative cruelty was publicized to establish that officer's individuality and earn recognition for personal creativity. And, in the spirit of making sure that personal creativity is given clear social recognition, it was enacted and reenacted frequently, in virtually identical form—just as a concert pianist plays his or her personal version of Mozart over and over again, at concert after concert. No amount of daily repetition was too much to demonstrate the SS officer's personal creativity and claim to unique accomplishments within the larger scheme of Auschwitz: the fulsome bureaucratized practice of evil.

The ways of cruelty at Auschwitz were so organized that individual contributions were not encroached upon by others. Each guard could cultivate his specialty with relative confidence that it would not be taken over by others. His "copyright," indicating his individuality, was honored. Just as he would honor the "copyright" of others, and just as in the wider world of art individual painters are protected against forgers who might copy their work.

All this required not only publicity, but a context—the *culture of cruelty*—in which creatively cruel deeds were acknowledged, valued, and rewarded precisely because they were cruel.

Hannnah Arendt observed the former Auschwitz officers at their trial in Frankfurt twenty years after the events happened. What she saw can be regarded as the culture of cruelty being remembered and relived. Arendt says:

One suspects the smiling reminiscences of the defendants, who listen delightedly to the recounting of deeds that occasionally make not only the witnesses but the jurors cry and faint; their incredible bows to those who bear testimony against them and recognize them, having once been their helpless victims; their open joy at being recognized [though incriminated] and hence remembered; and their usually high spirits throughout...here in the courtroom they all behave alike...[56]

Evidently the SS men took pride in getting renewed recognition for their creative contributions. They reacted as a former opera singer might, upon being told that you heard her singing at the Metropolitan Opera thirty-five years ago and that you will never forget her performance. She is apt to beam with delight, just as the former SS men beamed upon being reminded of their moments of creativity. The good feelings were rekindled in the ex-SS officer because the individual officer's creative contributions to the culture of cruelty, his "artistic" achievements, were once again remembered as the witnesses and prosecution vividly described them. The culture of cruelty that embodied the personal accomplishments of SS officers had survived in a dormant state, in the minds of both the victims and perpetrators of evil. Now, at the trial, it was reactivated and relived. The SS officers' creativity was once more acknowledged. This was a source of great satisfaction for these officers, far outweighing the likelihood that, having their actions revealed, they might go to prison.

All this suggests that the culture of cruelty was a powerful phenomenon among Auschwitz guards. It was a bond among them, as well as the source of profound personal satisfaction.

Self-Escalating Cruelty   Although much of the killing at Auschwitz was routinized, carried out on a large, mass-production basis using minimal emotional involvement on the part of the supervisory guards, killing also resulted from sudden explosions of unplanned acts of violence. It took place virtually every day, often generated by small, innocuous events within the system that quickly escalated to murderous levels. The escalating cruelty was usually generated entirely from within the system.

To begin with, Hoess, the chief of the camp, set an example. Hoess prided himself on being extremely "hard" and ruthless. Given his posture, the death penalty and extremes of torture were inflicted very readily—even upon SS colleagues, but most pervasively and commonly upon prisoners. With such a policy by the highest authority of the camp the lower officers and the Capos (prisoners who served as guards) followed the leader's example in practicing cruelty.

Hoess used the cruelty of his underlings to justify even more cruelty by himself. He reported that he became ever-more unfeeling and dictatorial when he saw the cruelty of his underlings. His own cruelty, in turn, created incentives for the underlings to practice even more cruelty. After all, their leader was their model. He personified the rules of the organization. In this way the system of cruelty-enhancement was self-escalating. Once begun, and in the absence of outside interruption, each act of cruelty created more cruelty. (Remember, too, that it continued even though its major practitioner, Hoess, was appalled by it!)

Hoess reported his own, personal process of escalation of cruelty. The war created many shortages, particularly of "good" personnel. The personnel he had angered him by their "indifference and sloppiness and lack of cooperation." But even before the onset of wartime shortages, the government in Berlin had been niggardly in giving him the sort of resources he felt he needed. Hoess reported that, given the many disappointments and disillusion, he "became a different person.... I became distrustful and highly suspicious..." He shunned all sociable contact with his colleagues. "All human emotions were forced into the background.... I had eyes only for my work."

The Auschwitz camp was a relatively closed system. (Hoess complained bitterly about the camp being too closed off from outside support.) Here self-escalating processes occurred readily and, with no outside forces to counteract them, often ended in the murder of an inmate. Cruelty sometimes began with innocuous little acts that could feed upon other acts and quickly escalate into major acts of cruelty. For example, a guard's minor irritation over an inmate's shoes might quickly lead to the inmate's death: The guard criticizes the inmate's shoes; the inmate does not immediately produce the expected abject apology; the guard pulls out his gun and shoots the inmate.

In this closed system there was no room for outside forces, such as an independent investigation into the inmate's supposed "infraction" of rules regarding shoes, to interrupt the process of escalation. The guard had the authority to escalate his responses, including making life-and-death decisions.

Although the practice of cruelty at Auschwitz was self-escalating, and very common, it was not all-pervasive. It had a distinct location in social space, it was enacted in specific zones.

"Zoned" Cruelty   Zoning of behavior is a crucial attribute of bureaucracies generally. It is used to nurture particular kinds of behavior and harness it to achieve the organization's objectives. Hospitals, for example, are bureaucratic organizations in which medical healing behavior is nurtured (encouraged, developed) and harnessed (put into use) so that it maximizes the treatment of sick patients. The process includes delineating clearly zoned areas where healing-behavior can take place—stipulating who may do it and who may not do it, what activities are appropriate and what activities are inappropriate, when it may take place and when it may not take place. Such zoning of behavior takes place in most bureaucracies. It also took place at Auschwitz. There zoning of behavior, geared to achieving that camp's murderous mission, took the form of zoning cruelty. It included the following features.

An SS officer could engage in limitless cruelty against inmates. But he could not be equally cruel toward his SS colleagues. To be sure, he was occasionally angry at a colleague, but he had to confine a cruel response to his dealings with inmates, since colleagues could not be tortured with impunity. Toward colleagues a "gentlemanly" code of conduct prevailed. Fellow-officers might be liked or disliked, esteemed or scorned, but one could not shoot them or push them into the gas chamber, unless the officer was proven to have committed an ultimate crime, such as helping a prisoner escape. Ordinarily, "gentlemanly" colleagueship prevailed.

In the Hoess family life, too, very different rules of conduct prevailed. There was consideration for others, a sense of respect for life and human decency. While a female camp inmate worked at the Hoess household as a maid, she came under these rules of conduct. While in the Hoess household she was not brutalized. Here the family-conduct rules dominated over camp-inmate conduct rules. But there was always a silent rider to the work of the maid in the Hoess household: At any moment she could be barred from the Hoess household and forced to return to being a regular camp inmate, with all the horrors that this entailed.

In short, cruelty was actively zoned, confined to behavior toward inmates. Even here, the cruel deeds were likely to happen in the specialized *zones of cruelty* that individual SS officers carved out for themselves. There were also *zones of immunity* from cruelty. Working in the Hoess household was one of these. Another was serving as a Capo, an assistant to SS officers in their ghoulish deeds. These zones of immunity were usually occupied temporarily, until the inmate's turn came to go back to the zone of regular inmate, subject to "regular" cruelty.

Although the cruel deeds at Auschwitz were virtually limitless in their ferocity, there were boundaries to the practice of cruelty: toward one category of person cruelty was clearly out of bounds. Boundaries also applied to the activities themselves. Acts of kindness toward prisoners were usually out of bounds. This ruled out acts of ordinary human decency—concern for human dignity, privacy, and life itself—as these are generally accepted in modern societies, even in German society during the Nazi era.

But it was not quite so simple. In fact, acts of kindness by SS officers toward Auschwitz prisoners did occasionally occur. They occurred under two circumstances:

- Under conditions of privacy, when no one else was around.
- Publicly, when they underscored that the SS officer knew good from evil, but was giving clear preference to evil. Typical of this pattern was the act of sending flowers and chocolates to a woman who had just given birth to a child and the next day sending her to the gas chambers. And so was the occasional, seemingly warm attentiveness to newly arrived prisoners at the Auschwitz railroad ramp, while getting them ready to be murdered. Prisoners were told they will take showers before they will be issued new clothes in preparation for going to work. They were sometimes handed soap to make it more convincing. (This technique also prevented prisoners from becoming panicky and attacking the SS personnel.)

Within its boundaries, Auschwitz developed ways of accentuating cruelty. One way of doing so was by fostering a climate of capriciousness within the confines of Auschwitz. The Auschwitz administration, from Commandant Hoess on down to the lowest guard, practiced their awful craft by confronting inmates with secrecy, unpredictability and arbitrariness. Largely out of bounds was giving inmates accurate information, some measure of predictability in their lives, and orderly procedures that made some sense. Instead, cruelty was accentuated by the capricious manner in which it was administered. The inmates were kept wondering, who will be murdered next? What new technique will they use? Such psychological torture, alongside the physical torture, was fair game within the Auschwitz zone of cruelty.

Finally, there was yet another form of zoning of cruelty. It applied especially to administrators of concentration camps. In some earlier research on organizations, such as hospitals, factories, and schools, it became clear that high administrative officials have much autonomy in some zones of behavior and virtually no autonomy in other zones. Specifically, they have a great deal of autonomy *within* their organizational roles, they can make all sorts of policy decisions, but they have relatively little autonomy outside their organizational role. They belong to their organization, body and soul. They can be enterprising and inventive within their organizational role. And they can derive rewards and personal satisfaction from this activity. But one thing they cannot engage in, cannot even entertain for consideration, is active alienation from their organizational role. They are not permitted to "step outside" and look at their organizational role from an outsider's perspective.

Hoess (and Stangl, as described by Gitta Sereny) expressed considerable alienation toward his role as concentration camp commandant after he was no longer in that role. Both Hoess and Stangl claimed that this alienation existed for many years. But before their incarceration, while they were still in their roles, they not only did not express such alienation, they performed their murderous role with zeal and imagination. They did not hold back but, instead, gave of themselves with the fullest dedication and commitment. During their interactions with their families, while in the camp commandant role, they never stepped outside their commandant role far enough to be actively and fundamentally critical of it. In short, the practice of cruelty was part of the commandant's role that was so zoned, so shielded from external censure, that even when the commandant physically left the camp to be with his family he was unable to even entertain any consideration of the horror of his deeds. He operated entirely within the zone of cruelty. If he was alienated from the cruelty of his role, that alienation was entirely shunted aside, remaining dormant among the components of his package of values and behaviors.

The Inventiveness of Bureaucrats   Parts of this book mention the inventiveness of individuals at creating new and ever-more horrifying evil deeds. Appalling as this is, it is probably not the most appalling inventiveness in the realm of evil. The most appalling feature may be the invention of a *mind-set* that regards outrageous evil as acceptable, even necessary, human behavior. Here I echo the thoughts of Robert Conquest (quoted at the beginning of this section) that perhaps the worst accomplishment of Stalin, even beyond his inflicting suffering that led to the death of around 14 million Ukrainians, was creation of a mind-set among bureaucratic functionaries that justified doing horrendously evil deeds.

Going a step beyond Robert Conquest's statement—that there is a mind-set that says outrageous evil is acceptable, even necessary, human behavior—one must acknowledge that this mind-set can occur among people who are not so demented that they do not recognize the difference between good and evil, and whose mental faculties, in many ways, have remained intact. People who are evidently quite sane can develop a mind-set that says it is appropriate to take part in what they themselves know to be massively murderous activity. How can this happen? How does this happen? To find answers, let us learn more from Hoess and Auschwitz. Let us take a close look to see how such a mind-set was actually created.

First, it was made possible by autonomy. Auschwitz officials were not mere robots. They did not carry out orders precisely as directed. They added to the orders. They detracted from the orders. They went around orders. They interpreted. They invented. To be able to do these things they, like other bureaucrats, used their own autonomy. They used it not only to invent evil deeds but to invent *justifications* for evil deeds with which they, individually, could live. In their minds they constructed an appropriate reality.

Second, autonomy, and the resulting inventiveness, existed among personnel at all levels, from Hoess on down to low-level functionaries. The SS officers on trial in Frankfurt had all been relatively low-ranking functionaries in the Auschwitz bureaucracy. Most of them had been guards of one sort or another. This means they were not "desk murderers," people who made administrative arrangements but did not personally kill people. Instead, these SS men had been the front line of evil. They had done the actual torturing, the killing. The trial testimony brought out that they were very innovative, using their autonomy to justify to themselves their part in the practice of cruelty.

In fairness, it must be noted that not all SS men at Auschwitz used their autonomy to justify participating in the culture of cruelty. Some used their autonomy to avoid participating in cruelty. For example, one newly arrived SS officer who, appalled by what he was expected to do, refused to take part in the cruelties and requested to be transferred out of Auschwitz. (He succeeded, and he was *not* punished for his refusal to participate in cruelties!) At least one SS officer—Oberscharfuehrer Flacke, in charge of the Bubice labor camp section—survivors reported, remained thoroughly decent throughout his years at Auschwitz.[57] These instances show that an SS officer's autonomy could be used to *not* take part in the culture of cruelty. But there were not many who did so. The majority used their inventiveness to create a niche for themselves within the culture of cruelty. There the practice of cruelty made them part of a rewarding system of social relationships. This justified doing evil, at least in part.

As I described previously, this applies mainly to fairly low-level members of an organization, such as the guards at Auschwitz. But how about the administrators, the bureaucratic chieftains, how do they justify their participation in evil? Do they not require a rather explicit mind-set that justifies their role in creating and supervising evil? Hoess, the commandant of Auschwitz, provides us with a cogent example of someone with just such a mind-set.

A startling feature about Hoess (and, perhaps, others) is that he retained a sense of revulsion against the Auschwitz cruelties but still took part in them fully and unreservedly.

While learning his trade of concentration camp administrator, Hoess used his own autonomy to work out the idea that revulsion was a necessary part of carrying out the package of duties to which he was committed. He persuaded himself that revulsion cannot be avoided and that, in fact, it serves a useful purpose.

Indeed, in Hoess's acceptance of his own evildoing, revulsion became the supreme catalyst.

Hoess derived some of his thinking from the previously mentioned speech by Heinrich Himmler, the head of the SS and a senior member of Hitler's inner circle. Himmler said that the slaughter of people carried out by the SS was indeed horrible and understandably a source of revulsion. But the slaughter was necessary, even laudable, because it was carried out on behalf of a very noble cause. The very revulsion proved the grandeur of one's contributions. Hence Hoess was not alone. The head of the SS promoted the same mind-set as the one Hoess adopted.

Many well-intentioned persons assume that if one creates enough revulsion about evil then such evil will not be repeated. Indeed, much of the effort to prevent future Holocausts rests on the following assumption: if the world will realize how horrible the Holocaust deeds were it will, then, not engage in them in the future. Hoess's mind-set casts doubt about the validity of this assumption.

In Hoess's mind-set revulsion is not denied; in fact it is accepted. It serves to tell Hoess that he is linked to an awesome and superior cause, one for which one must be prepared to sacrifice one's humane sensibilities. And this act of sacrifice underscores the worth, the grandeur, of that superior cause. Through this process of reasoning revulsion becomes the catalyst that enables one's participation in horrors to be regarded as acceptable behavior.

Let me summarize the steps involved, in the case of Hoess, at least, in creating the mind-set that justified taking part in horrendous evil:

1. Not only do the top leaders, the Hitlers and Stalins, have autonomy, which they use to devise schemes of horrendous evil, but underlings, too, have autonomy.

2. The underlings, from Hoess on down to the lowliest guard, use their autonomy to devise a mind-set to enable them to take part in evil and still live with themselves; that is, to still adhere to some semblance of a civil morality to which they have previously been exposed, while nonetheless taking part in evil.

3. Crucial to the process of creating the mind-set is the role of revulsion. Revulsion is accepted as a necessary price for

contributing to a grand cause. Revulsion is the catalyst that makes the system work. It tells Hoess that feeling revulsion means that he is still a human being, because to feel revulsion means that he is still capable of feeling. It also tells Hoess that renouncing something that means something to him—namely, the human sensibilities aroused by the feeling of revulsion—elevates the cause he is serving.

How valid is it to focus on the evil-justifying mind-set of one individual, such as Hoess? First, as already mentioned, Hoess' mind-set was shared and promoted by Heinrich Himmler, the chief of the entire SS organization. Himmler doubtless influenced many SS officers in that same direction. Second, Hoess, as head of the largest extermination camp, wielded great influence on the functionaries under him and, of course, on the millions of victims. His personal mind-set had enormous impact.

Finally, I do not claim that the sense of revulsion is the only possible catalyst for producing an evil-justifying mind-set. For Hoess it was seemingly the crucial catalyst. For other persons, under other circumstances, other items may have the dubious honor of being crucial catalysts to the production of an evil-justifying mind-set.

A Postscript to the Bureaucratic Way: The Bureaucrat and the Antibureaucrat—A Comparison of Rudolf Hoess and Raoul Wallenberg

Raoul Wallenberg was a young Swedish diplomat when, during the Second World War, his government sent him to Hungary to attempt to save some Jews from Nazi persecution. Wallenberg managed to frustrate the Nazi bureaucracy, and he personally succeeded in saving around 100,000 Jews. He stands in stark contrast to Rudolf Hoess, whose personal efforts—within a bureaucratic mode of action—organized the death of around 2 million Jews.

Wallenberg, who came from an upper-class Swedish family, had a very cosmopolitan upbringing. He spoke Swedish, French, English, Russian, and German. He traveled widely. His background (package) included a Jewish great-grandfather and business associations and friendships with Jewish refugees who had fled to Sweden after Hitler had come to power in Germany.

Shortly before Wallenberg was sent on his mission to help Jews in Hungary, he saw the movie *Pimpernel Smith* (based on *The Scarlet Pimpernel*). In that movie a British aristocrat (dashingly played by Leslie Howard) entered France and managed to save several persons whose lives were in danger from a repressive political regime. He did it by outwitting the regime's bureaucratic officials. Wallenberg, on his way home from seeing the movie, remarked to a friend that he wished he could be like the Scarlet Pimpernel.[58] This vision may well have become a rider to the situation in which Wallenberg found himself in Hungary, defining the situation as one in which the individual can overcome a bureaucracy. His subsequent actions, in outwitting the Nazis to save Jews, were in some ways very similar to those of the Scarlet Pimpernel.

Upon arriving in Hungary, Wallenberg proved to be innovative and resourceful, never flustered by Nazi threats, repeatedly inventing ways to help Jews escape from seemingly certain departure to the death camps. He accomplished much through quick-witted, incremental decisions that effectively overcame obstacles in the immediate context. He repeatedly defeated bureaucratic impediments. For instance, when Nazi bureaucrats claimed that the Jews were Hungarian citizens, and therefore outside of Sweden's jurisdiction, Wallenberg furnished Swedish passports to thousands of these Jews, thereby conferring Swedish state protection upon them. Wallenberg's actions displayed adroit use of his autonomy to address himself to a large issue, the threat posed by the Nazis' full-scale attack on human life.

For Hoess, that large issue was a very distant matter. It was far outweighed by immediate bureaucratic considerations. Hoess's autobiography suggests that he, too, regarded mass killing of human beings as wrong, even horrendous (these are his own words). But it was a very distant matter, far less important than obeying instructions from Berlin headquarters that demanded focusing on solving logistical problems in the day-to-day administration of the camp, including those involved in the extermination program.

For Wallenberg, on the other hand, the larger consideration, the massive attack on human life, was something to be addressed directly. In his thinking, obstacles in the form of immediate bureaucratic considerations were easily brushed aside in favor of a larger value, preserving human life. In the best sense, he had the aristocrat's luxury of being able to address himself to large issues and doing so in a very direct and practical way.

On the other hand, Hoess, this insecure bureaucratic functionary, concentrated entirely on immediacies. To him the "little" problems, within the bureaucracy, became big problems, filling his entire field of vision—and producing moral myopia of an extraordinary sort. Hoess managed to live with himself—with his conscience, with his upbringing—because ultimate values about the sanctity of life, to which he was exposed in childhood, were not explicitly abandoned. They were merely relegated to the background, giving way to concentrating on the immediate issues in the bureaucracy.

An incongruous fact is that Hoess and Wallenberg both believed in the sanctity of human life. But the two differed in the manner in which the sanctity of human life was packaged. For Wallenberg, it was the dominant element in his package, and a rider—derived from an aristocratic life style—told him that he could overcome immediate bureaucratic obstacles when human life was threatened. For Hoess, it was a very minor part of his package, based on the rider that Jews were subhuman and a danger to the German people's grand destiny. As a result, for Wallenberg, preserving the life of the victims became his immediate concern, that surpassed all others. For Hoess, on the other hand, preserving the life of the victims was an irrelevant issue, far surpassed by immediate bureaucratic issues.

Hoess and Wallenberg may not be at all unique. Indeed, they may exemplify real, although distinctly different ways of participating in a social order. Research findings by social scientists Melvin Kohn, Herbert Kelman and Lee Hamilton point in this direction.[59] In extensive studies of social strata Kohn found that persons located in the middle and upper strata place considerable emphasis on the individual's thinking for oneself. This contrasted with persons located in the working classes whose emphasis is on conforming to existing regulations. For the latter, especially, one's occupation—one's job—is a critical factor in shaping the social circumstances in which one finds oneself, and in how one goes about meeting day-to-day challenges.

Similarly, in survey studies Kelman and Hamilton found different, but clearly patterned, attitudes toward obeying unjust authority. They found

- A "rule orientation," focused on adhering to instructions in rather unquestioning ways, usually (but not always) operating among working classes;

- A "role orientation," focused on meeting the requirements of one's job, usually (but not always) operating among middle classes and, as in the case of the rule orientation, leading individuals to obey authorities unquestioningly, even when orders from these authorities have immoral content;

- A "value orientation," focused on taking personal responsibility for the consequences of one's actions, usually (but not always) operating among persons in authority and control positions.

These orientations correspond roughly to social class differences, although Kelman and Hamilton reject the claim by some scholars that there exists a distinctive "lower-class authoritarianism."

Wallenberg personifies the individual thinking for oneself, found often (but not exclusively) among members of the upper social strata. Hoess personifies the individual whose thinking is shaped by his or her occupational niche, who does not question work-related orders he or she knows to be immoral.

Hoess and Wallenberg responded very differently to immediate issues confronting them. Responding to immediate issues was also a major ingredient in the actions of Lt. William Calley at My Lai. This will now be examined.

MY LAI

"I vowed that if I survived the war in Vietnam I would tell the truth about war.... What do soldiers fight for?... They fight for their buddies."

—A Marine Corps General,
briefing American troops in the Persian Gulf.
(Cited on American ABC television, January 27, 1991)

When this book was still in manuscript form, a number of readers advised me not to include the section on My Lai. I was told that Americans have heard enough about that unhappy event. And, I was told, it should not be placed in the same book with a discussion of Auschwitz. I agree that Auschwitz is evil of an entirely different order of magnitude from any other evil that has thus far been perpetrated. Certainly My Lai is a far lesser evil than Auschwitz.

Yet My Lai was an event where evil things happened. I am including it not because I want to drive yet another nail into the coffin of that unhappy chapter in American history, the war in Vietnam. I bring it up here neither to condemn that war nor to justify it. I bring it up to learn something valuable from it.

The My Lai events demonstrate in a unique and critical way how, at a particular point in time and space, a context can so mold persons, temporarily at least, that they will engage in activities that go entirely against the grain of their own upbringing. Persons who, to the best of our knowledge, were entirely decent, well-brought-up human beings, one day slaughtered hundreds of innocent people, and they did so with joy. I include their story, not because I believe these persons were different from the rest of us but, on the contrary, because they were probably very much like the rest of us. Not only are the American soldiers who served in Vietnam our kinspeople, our sons and daughters, our brothers and sisters, our fathers and mothers. In their makeup they are us. They are ourselves. And so, too, are the particular soldiers who were in My Lai on May 16, 1968. We cannot distance ourselves from these soldiers. In them we are obliged to confront a side of our own human nature that really exists.

By looking at this side we find that our human nature is rather flexible and, when pushed, can produce some nasty results. Still, this is a part of what we are. And we had better learn what we are.

In an unanticipated way, My Lai is giving us a gift of knowledge about our maleability, our ability to be flexible as we adapt to situations in which we find ourselves.

One Day in an American Soldier's Career: The My Lai Massacre

On the morning of March 16, 1968, American soldiers operating in the hamlet of My Lai 4 of South Vietnam massacred innocent villagers. The massacre lasted about three hours. It ended just before noon, when the soldiers took a lunch break. By then between 450 and 500 old men, children, babies, and women of all ages were dead. Most of them had been rounded up, herded together into groups, and killed by automatic rifle fire. But at least one old man had been killed individually, as he was found cowering in his domicile; at least one woman had been killed individually, after being molested by soldiers; at least one baby had been killed individually as it, uncomprehendingly, held onto its slaughtered mother's breast.

At Auschwitz, Dr. Kremer and Commandant Hoess were aware that they were taking part in evil. But their packages, their behavior frameworks, were so organized that their evil deeds were treated as entirely secondary, having given way to other priorities within their respective packages.

On the other hand, Lieutenant William Calley, who led the platoon that carried out the acts at My Lai, had no awareness that he was taking part in evil. And he, apparently, was not alone in feeling this way. Here was a situation where the practice of evil became morally invisible to the participants in it. Here immediacy prevailed (just as it did in the Milgram laboratory experiments) to the extent that values of the larger society, on which each of the participants had been raised, became irrelevant. The local construction of reality dominated entirely. It consisted of a package that contained specific predisposing items (such as the body count emphasis) and specific catalysts (such as the death by ambush of a well-liked sergeant). But above all, a rider emerged that defined the killing as a festive occasion. This rider permeated the entire event, giving Marines the autonomy to kill with joy and abandon.

Evil became morally invisible because, for some hours, an abbreviated culture of cruelty reigned. Here cruelty was enjoyed precisely because it was cruel. Yet it was an "abbreviated" culture of cruelty because there was no time for specialized roles in cruelty to emerge and become stabilized, as happened at Auschwitz. There was no time for individuals to gain a reputation for repeatedly enacting a particular form of cruelty. But there was joy in acting cruelly and, for a flickering moment providing a rewarding forum for cruelty, there flourished an exuberant culture of cruelty.

Charlie Company (in which Lieutenant Calley served as a platoon leader) was assigned the task of attacking My Lai. The attack was orchestrated as a *full-fledged battle*. The night before the attack the soldiers were briefed by their officers to expect that on this, their first major encounter with the enemy, they would receive heavy opposition. The high military echelons, at the battalion and division levels, were so convinced that there would be a major military action that they alerted the army's media to cover the action, from helicopters and from the ground. In addition, high-ranking officers from the brigade and division levels were allocated air space, so that they, too, might observe the battle's progress from helicopters.

Immediately before the Marine assault a heavy barrage of artillery shells was laid down on what would be the battle zone. During their descent, in their helicopters, the Marines began to open fire. After reaching the ground they secured the landing area and quickly proceeded to advance upon the village, firing full blast all the time.

It took them some time to realize that there was no return fire. There was no military response to the Marines. There were no enemy soldiers at My Lai, only women, old men, and young children. It is not clear whether military intelligence had been faulty—that there had not been any enemy military forces at My Lai at all—or whether the enemy's military forces escaped shortly before the Marines arrived. What is clear is that no military forces were at My Lai 4 during the Marine assault. What is also clear is that the Marines honestly expected a full-fledged battle. They expected to do battle with an enemy who would be there to fight. This was one ingredient in the Marines' package of expectations.

Another expectation centered on the *body count*. The Vietnam War was a strange war. It gave rise to a strange accounting system, the body count, mentioned earlier. "Ordinary" wars, in the past, had their share of confusion. But at least it was usually fairly clear where the battle lines were drawn, where one's own sector ended and where the enemy's sector began, which piece of land was "ours" and which was "theirs." It was clear, above all, who the enemy was and who one's friends were. All this was different in Vietnam, which was a guerilla war. It refused to adhere to the "rules" of warfare. Battle lines were extremely fluid. The enemy was here today and gone tomorrow, to pop up somewhere else, perhaps in front of you, perhaps behind your lines. Friends and foe were hard to distinguish. Neither spoke English.

Here the traditional indicators of military success had little value. One could not point to so many square miles of land captured today when, the next day, the enemy appeared in your own rear areas. In this situation there emerged, on the American side, a new way to measure military success: the body count, the number of enemy soldiers killed. This was used as a major indicator of military performance. High military officers insisted on receiving the daily body count. It was recorded. It was widely publicized. It was used to measure the effectiveness of individual military units and the performance of individual officers.

In any war it is difficult to know how many persons are killed, be they military or civilian. In a guerrilla war it is doubly difficult. To solve the problem military personnel become inventive. They make up figures, especially when the stakes are high because officers are being evaluated by the criterion of how many enemy soldiers their units have killed. In Vietnam the military also became careless as to whether they were counting enemy soldiers or civilians. After all, the enemy did not wear proper uniforms to identify itself. And it was difficult to tell, the Marines reported, whether an old lady did not hide a grenade or whether a young child was not about to join the guerrillas.

The result was a flourishing economy of body count statistics. Military units would out-do one another in body count claims. Frequently the number of enemy soldiers claimed to have been killed bore no relation to the reality that existed on the battleground. And the distinction between soldiers and unarmed, innocent civilians was often ignored. Lieutenant Calley regarded body count as partly a joke, because he knew that they were often simply invented. Yet he also regarded body count with some awe because he knew that his superiors used it to evaluate him and his men. For him, and for his fellow-Marines, producing a high body count was important. It was a tangible item in their package of expectations at My Lai.

The third component in the Marines' package leading up to the My Lai events emerged from the fact that seemingly all their expectations were being frustrated. The war the American soldier encountered in Vietnam produced a great deal of *fury and frustration.* Lieutenant Calley reported:[60]

> One night they captured one of us. I heard the GI scream all night.... We listened and we just cringed! At dawn we went to the high poles that he had been strung on. His skin had been ripped from his arms, legs, abdomen: ...What in the hell's happening? We had better be winning or this wasn't worth it. Death and death. And more death.
>
> And that's what the thing was. We weren't winning in South Vietnam...we were men in a pond pushing away the water...and as fast as we pushed it away it rushed in.[61]

For Lieutenant Calley's Charlie Company much of the fury and frustration reached a crescendo just before it began its action at My Lai. A number of men had been killed or wounded in ambushes, the victims of "unfair" ways of conducting war, where the American soldiers rarely saw the enemy and even more rarely managed to punish the enemy for these deeds.

In the weeks preceding the action at My Lai, gradually, incrementally, "the men of Charlie Company were getting more violent," reported Seymour Hersh after 250 interviews with former members of the company.[62] One soldier said: "First, you'd stop the people, question them, and let them go; Second, you'd stop the people, beat up an old man, and let them go; Third, you'd stop the people, beat up an old man, and then shoot him. Fourth, you go in and wipe out a village."[63]

On the very day Charlie Company received orders for the My Lai action they held funeral services for Sergeant Cox. Cox had been killed by a booby trap. He had been very well liked. The funeral ceremony contained the customary rituals: a prayer recited by the chaplain; and some words by the captain, the company's commander. Lieutenant Calley reported that he and the others were greatly "stirred up" by Cox's death.[64] It doubtless heightened the fury and frustration in the package that made up the outlook of members of Charlie Company.

Above all, the My Lai action had an aura of festivity. Indeed, *festivity* became the dominant rider to the My Lai actions of the Marines. The killings were carried out in a spirit of joy. Here is an eye witness account. It was reported by Seymour Hersh, who, several months after My Lai occurred, interviewed two men who were sent by "the Army's 31st Public Information Department to record the event [the great anticipated battle] for history."[65] The men were Jay Roberts, a reporter, and Ronald L. Haeberle, a photographer. They reached My Lai with the second wave of helicopters.

> Roberts and Haeberle...moved in just behind the third platoon. Haeberle watched a group of ten to fifteen GIs methodically pump bullets into a cow until it keeled over. A woman then poked her head out from behind some brush; she may have been hiding in a bunker. The GIs turned their fire from the cow to the woman. "They just kept shooting at her. You could see the bones flying in the air chip by chip." No one had attempted to

question her; GIs inside the hamlet also were asking no questions. Before moving on, the photographer took a picture of the dead woman. Haeberle took many more pictures that day; he saw about thirty GIs kill at least a hundred Vietnamese civilians.

When the two correspondents entered My Lai 4, they saw dead animals, dead people, burning huts and houses. A few GIs were going through victims' clothing looking for piasters. Another GI was chasing a duck with a knife; others stood around watching a GI slaughter a cow with a bayonet.

As Haeberle and Roberts walked further into the hamlet Medina [the commanding officer of Charlie Company, Captain Ernest L. Medina] came up to them. Eighty-five Viet Cong had been killed in action thus far, the captain told them, and twenty suspects had been captured.[66] Roberts carefully jotted down the captain's statistics in his notepad.... Now it was nearly nine o'clock and all of Charlie Company was in My Lai 4. Most families were being shot inside their homes, or just outside the doorways. Those who had tried to flee were crammed by GIs into the many bunkers built throughout the hamlet for protection—once the bunkers became filled, hand grenades were lobbed in. Everything became a target. [One soldier]...borrowed someone's M79 grenade launcher and fired it point-blank at a water buffalo: "I hit that sucker right in the head; went down like a shot. You don't get to shoot water buffalo with an M79 every day." Others fired the weapon into the bunkers full of people.[67]

From other interviews with former GIs Hersh reported: "some GIs were shouting and yelling during the massacre: 'The boys enjoyed it. When someone laughs and jokes about what they're doing, they have to be enjoying it.' A GI said, 'Hey, I got me another one.' Another said, 'Chalk up one for me.'"[68] Killing was done in a festive mood.

Not all GIs joined in the festive killing. For example, one GI deliberately shot himself in the leg so that he would not need to continue to participate. Another, a helicopter pilot, tried to intervene to stop the massacre. He succeeded in rescuing a few persons.

But the GIs who did not participate in the festive killing were in the minority. Many of the others, probably the majority, did participate. They did it with exuberance. They were having fun. Festivity was a prominent ingredient in the My Lai package.

Months later when Lieutenant Calley received orders to

return to the United States he was not told that he was going to stand trial for the deeds at My Lai. He thought he was ordered back to receive a medal. He had been an obedient Marine. And My Lai had received much favorable publicity in Army circles. It had produced a high body count. It had been declared to be a huge military success.

Summary: The My Lai Package and Its Dominant Rider

The various component items of the Marines' package did not remain separate and independent of each other. They came together and formed a synthesis, a way of organizing and making sense out of it all. And the synthesis spelled out a course of action for the Marines at My Lai.

In the immediate situation at My Lai the Marines' package included the expectation of a military confrontation, the frustration of a regular Marine unit having to fight a guerilla war for which it was not adequately trained and the body count economics governing many of their activities. These items in the Marines' package required only a catalyst to create a synthesis among all the items. The synthesis, when it came, spelled out a concrete course of action. It told the Marines how they were to get on with their My Lai assignment, how they were to act in their confrontation with the people of My Lai. The catalyst was provided by the death by booby trap of the popular Sergeant Cox and, after the My Lai action started, by the prodding administered to Lieutenant Calley by his superior officer, to get his men moving and not be such a persistent "loser" in the fine art of doing battle and manufacturing body count: dead bodies were needed.

Once the My Lai action began, there emerged a festive air to the random killing, which added to the momentum. What sparked it I do not know. But, once started, festivity became a new element in the My Lai package. Indeed, the festive character of the killing became the dominant, all-pervasive element in the package. It set the tone. It became a fundamental rider to all activities. It prescribed exuberant killing. It amounted to telling the Marine: You encounter a young child—You kill it! You meet a feeble old man—You kill him! There is satisfaction, even joy, in killing!

This synthesis organized the Marines' social reality. It prescribed a course of action in response to the frustration and confusion the Marines had experienced. It gave them a sense of potency, of finally doing something that seemed to make a difference. It gave them release and fulfillment.

For the My Lai Marine, the *festive killing rider* guided every act. It did not tell him specifically what to do. It merely oriented his perspective. Thus, it showed him how to react to a young Vietnamese child, to an old man, to a nursing mother. Whether he then pulled the trigger of his gun or used his bayonet was within his zone of discretion. He had autonomy to decide for himself which mode of killing he would use. But how he looked at the villagers, his perspective, was given to him by the rider that permeated his thinking while he walked through the village of My Lai. That rider gave him the license to kill and the incentive to kill indiscriminately.

In My Lai the festive killing rider prevailed among the majority (but not all) of the Marines. Years later, bereft of this particular context and influenced by the anti-war movement of the early 1970s, many a GI questioned the legitimacy of that rider. New riders emerged and dominated during the 1970s. Then, under the Reagan administration as of 1981, there emerged once again a new set of priorities about the Vietnam war, including massacres such as those at My Lai. To be sure, no one applauded massacres. But new riders, new dominating judgments, were formulated and began to permeate the evaluation of the part played by American troops in that war. These interpretations emphasized a more positive view of the American contribution to the Vietnam war. New riders were at work.

Calley was personally caught in the change of riders. During his period of training as a Marine there was no question that a Marine-machismo rider dominated. It demanded that he learn to be an effective killer of enemies and obey all orders from his superiors. By the time he stood trial, Calley faced a mounting antiwar milieu. The new dominant rider was a profound disillusionment about American participation in the Vietnam war. In the years since his trial, Calley and others like him became the objects of an even newer rider, a rider that stated "the American troops in Vietnam were just doing their duty."

In short, new riders can emerge and displace old ones, resulting in attributing new meanings to, and making new evaluations of, the same events. Today's evil is tomorrow's good deed. Killers may get medals. But the dead remain dead. No reinterpretation of history will bring them back to life. Traditionally we have adapted to this stark reality by eventually persuading ourselves that the deaths were not in vain, that they were noble sacrifices. (Recall, this is what the people in my Bavarian village did.) Yet there can be another adaptation. We can try to turn away from doing evil.

CHAPTER 4

Conclusion: Turning away from Evil

Most of this book has focused on how easy it is to take part in evil—on how very ordinary social behaviors can contribute to evil, on how it takes so very little deviation from everyday activities to contribute to evil, and that we need to learn how the process of creating evil works. But the book has also mentioned persons who resisted evil—persons who used ordinary human social behavior to not take part in evil. From them we can learn something about resisting evil. Let us return to them. Then, reconsider the five paradoxes, but this time from the point of view of avoiding evil. Next, examine the larger picture, including some potentials for evil embedded in the makeup of modern society. Finally, a look at lessons we are learning from the preceding pages as we overcome our ignorance of how evil is produced and as we move toward a new freedom, the freedom of mastery over evil.

But first, a small digression.

A FABLE ABOUT THE
TWO RESEARCH-MINDED PHYSICIANS

If Dr. Doe and Dr. Kremer had met at a medical research conference in a peaceful setting, let us say in Switzerland in the year 1950; and if Dr. Doe had not heard of Dr. Kremer's Auschwitz activities and Dr. Kremer did not volunteer to supply this bit of information about himself; then they might well have found that they had much in common. They could relate to each other very readily. They had a great deal to talk about. After all, they were both passionate medical researchers. Although each had rather specific research interests, they found common topics quickly enough, including a distaste for having to spend time with patients when they would have preferred to spend their time on their research and a common feeling that clinical medical colleagues were frequently a rather dimwitted lot, who did not really understand the researcher's sense of commitment to research or, even, how the researcher actually thinks.

After a few drinks together the two felt increasingly brotherly, sharing the frustrations of the medical researcher trying to live up to that calling—the search for fundamental discoveries that would make a real difference in the diagnosis and treatment of disease—in the face of a world that forced them to deal with locally pressing, but uninteresting, medical matters, like tending to bedside care of patients. After a few more drinks Dr. Kremer lost some of his restraint and started to talk about the pity that Hitler had lost the war, that they should have finished the job of killing the Jews. At that point something dawned in Dr. Doe's mind, although on him, too, the drinks had left their mark. He asked Dr. Kremer, "Who did you say you are?" "Where were you during the war?" And before hearing the full answer, he suddenly knew the answer, drunk though he was. And, in very uncharacteristic fashion, for he was usually the mildest of men, he clenched his right fist, reared back and socked Dr. Kremer in the jaw.

In real life these two men never met. They followed very different scientific careers. As I mentioned earlier, they had much in common—in their commitment to medical research, in their actual day-to-day medical research activities, in the package of behavior that made up their posture toward their medical career. Yet Dr. Kremer fully embraced the evils of Nazism and Dr. Doe remained a thoroughly humane human being. Dr. Doe's life contained some very instructive elements about resisting evil.

Was Dr. Doe tempted by evil? He certainly was. He told me (and I had been aware before he told me) that he earned far less than pathologists in many other hospitals. Medical pathologists in different hospitals, although doing roughly comparable work, tend to work under different financial and administrative arrangements (whether, for example, they receive a fixed salary or a fee for each service they render to a patient). These arrangements can influence the size of their income as well as their professional activities, including how they react when they discover unnecessary surgery. Dr. Doe continued to accept his arrangement because, in his words, "It lets me do the best job for patients." He was not criticizing other pathologists, who work under different arrangements. He was merely saying that he felt *he* could not do the best possible job for patients if he worked under a different arrangement. Therefore he stayed with the work arrangement that gave him a relatively low income. He acted on the belief that the dignity of the patient demands the best possible medical treatment.[1] And this, in turn, demands a rather selfless commitment to what one knows is the best service one can render. For Dr. Doe, and his family, this required financial sacrifices.

Another instance of temptation by evil occurred in connection with the availability of a new piece of technology, the electronmicroscope.[2] Ordinarily pathologists make their diagnoses by examining tissue which has been removed during operations and during autopsies. They do so in their laboratory, using the naked eye to examine how the tissue looks from the outside, and they use a microscope to examine tissue more minutely. Under magnification of the microscope they can see structures and ongoing processes that are not visible to the naked eye. With the advent of the electronmicroscope came the opportunity to magnify many thousands of times more than was possible with the regular microscope.

Along with the electronmicroscope came a curious new dilemma about *time*. With the electronmicroscope one can observe changes that might take years to show up on the more gross level of the regular microscope, not to mention how long it would take to show up to the naked eye. That is, at the level at which the electronmicroscope "sees," changes take place vastly more rapidly than they would at a lesser level of magnification. Hence, it now seemed imperative that the examination be made very early if one did not want to miss a vast amount of change that can take place even in a few minutes. In relation to patients who have died it seemed that the examination by electronmicroscope should be made at the bedside, immediately upon death, if one wanted to take advantage of this technological tool for discovering the cause of death more accurately. It would mean performing an autopsy, perhaps only a partial autopsy, on the deceased immediately upon death.

Dr. Doe mentioned this issue to me—he brought it up; I had not heard of an electronmicroscope. He did so with a sense of distaste, indicating the emotional hurt it would inflict on relatives of the deceased who were likely to be close by. To them it was surely an additional shock to immediately be confronted with an autopsy being performed on their loved one. Despite Dr. Doe's own commitment to scientific research he placed priority on the human factor, in this case the emotional state of the bereaved family members and the protection of their sensitivities and rights—their dignity. And yet he was tempted. Remember, he was the one who brought up the issue of the electronmicroscope.

His response to the temptation was to put human dignity ahead of using the latest item of technical equipment for making medical diagnosis. But he did so fully aware that it was done at a cost. Evil was not avoided automatically. It was avoided by conscious decision, by deliberate choice among competing priorities.

In a broader sense, Dr. Doe operated under the overarching rider that preserving a measure of human dignity has priority above all else. It colored all his activities and all his choices as a physician. Dr. Kremer, by contrast, accepted the Nazi rider that some people were not human at all; that the Nazi leadership could designate the people who come under this classification; and hence, that such people as Jews, Gypsies, mental defectives, Soviet prisoners-of-war, and political leaders captured in Poland were all regarded as less than human, and could be killed at will. It is difficult to see how an educated person, a scientist, could accept that Nazi rider. But Dr. Kremer, and many others, did accept it.

A lesson is apparent here. Dr. Doe demonstrates that the dignity-of-human-life rider can have fundamental and practical impact on the capacity to resist evil. It can place a distinctive coloration on an entire package of behavior so that, as in the case of Drs. Kremer and Doe, virtually the same package of behaviors will be interpreted differently, depending on whether this rider is accepted.

RAOUL WALLENBERG AND RUDOLF HOESS REVISITED

"One of the marvels of the human mind is the ability to make our lives into stories we can live with, where against all odds we emerge as heroes."

George Johnson

Perhaps you considered it preposterous that, earlier in the book, I compared Raoul Wallenberg, that heroic Swedish diplomat who singlehandedly saved some 100,000 persons from almost certain death, with Rudolf Hoess, the man in charge of the Auschwitz extermination camp who personally designed many of the extermination procedures and who supervised the annihilation of around 2 million persons.

I claimed that both men had an early upbringing that emphasized the sanctity of human life. For Wallenberg this value was a dominant item in his immediate and ongoing behavior; it was the dominant rider that permeated all his efforts while he intervened on behalf of the Jews of Hungary. For Hoess the sanctity-of-human-life value, though never completely renounced, was relegated to the background; it became secondary to other considerations within his package.

For the unfortunate victims of Hoess's deeds it made no difference whether he had renounced the sanctity-of-human-life value or merely placed it in a very subordinate position in his personal package of values. But for Hoess, personally, it made a great deal of difference. By placing that value in a subordinate position, and not explicitly renouncing it, he could continue to tell himself that he was still a sensitive and humane person, still the same person he had always been. His sense of self remained intact through this mechanism of making up a life story with which he could live.

My first inclination was to regard Hoess's claim—that he retained the sanctity-of-human-life value, but merely relegated it to the background—as a piece of pure fiction that should be dismissed. But Hoess's ongoing family life while he served as chief of Auschwitz demonstrates that for him, as he personally saw it, it was not a fiction. It was real to himself. In his own family he did practice humane values! On this basis he was able to continue to live with himself, and retain a sense of himself as a sensitive and humane person, while openly trampling on the sanctity-of-human-life value in his daily activities at the Auschwitz camp. Without the convenient prop to his sense of self—without this "doubling," as Robert Lifton calls it—would he have been able to sustain his level of evildoing? I doubt it. But I am not sure.

From the Wallenberg-Hoess comparison there are lessons to be learned for turning away from evil:

- Persons may share humane values, but behave in entirely different ways when it comes to implementing these values. For example, a male student from a fundamentalist non-

Western country studying at an American university, may genuinely accept American values about women's rights to equality. But upon returning to his own country that value may be displaced by other values and be relegated to the background.

- Persons may sincerely believe in a value, such as the sanctity of human life, but give it very low priority among their other, competing values. An illustrative phenomenon, of the dominance of one value over other values, exists in the case of General Robert E. Lee at the time of the American Civil War. Apparently Lee believed neither in slavery nor in secession. Yet he led the Confederate army, which attempted to attain secession and perpetuation of slavery. And he did so with the greatest of zeal, courage, and dedication. He did so because his package of values was dominated by one value, which became a rider to all his activities: the sense of commitment to his region, to Virginia in particular.[3]

The priorities among the values within one's package of values makes a great deal of difference in how one behaves.

Stated differently, we are not very likely to encounter persons who are thoroughgoing monsters, who have no humane values at all in their makeup. It is far more likely that we encounter people—in every society, in every stratum, in every group, in every community—who share many humane values with us. But they can differ considerably from us in the place these values occupy within their own package of behavior. Within their package humane values may occupy an utterly secondary place, or they may be prominent and dominant.

This tells us something about ourselves. To steer away from evil it is crucial that we recognize what *place* we allocate to humane values within our own makeup: where are they located within our personal package? It is not enough to believe in certain particular values. We need to know where these values stand among our own habits, among our own commitments, among our competing interests.

Translating these abstract thoughts about values into actual behavior, we must ask, How do we really operate when we have to make difficult choices? What do we do when we have to choose between accepting a financially attractive career opportunity and loyalty to a dear one; when we have to choose between honestly revealing the entire truth about a particular situation when we know this would be costly to ourselves; when we go along with love for the political scoundrel who is our country's ally; and so on. By answering such questions we can discover the location that our values actually occupy within our personal package.

I am not saying that we must at all times choose to accept a particular value, such as the sanctity of human life, or the importance of human dignity. I am not trying to dictate what our values and priorities should be. But it would be a great help to know just how less-than-noble, if not outright evil, dispositions are embedded in our makeup. This kind of knowledge about our behavior makeup is surely as important as knowing our genetic makeup.

As a nation we are currently going to great and expensive lengths to discover the content and structure—and potentials for pathology—of genetic codes under which we operate. This is to be applauded. But we surely need to know, far more accurately than we do now, the behavioral codes (what I call packages) under which we also operate. And this requires knowing not only the content—which values—make up our behavioral codes. It also requires knowing how these values are structured—organized, arranged—within these codes. (The revolutionary discoveries of DNA principles are also focused on the structure—the organization, the arrangement—of genetic materials.)

I do not claim that our value packages are permanently fixed and unchangeable (as genetic codes were thought to be before the advent of genetic engineering); that behaviorally we are doomed to accept and live by our existing behavioral structures. But before we can make changes we need to know which values we have and, at least equally important, the ways in which they are in fact structured within the packages that make up our behavioral codes.

Knowing the structure of our packages includes knowing which items within a package are dominant and which are subordinate; which items are active and which are dormant, awaiting activation when appropriate stimuli come along.[4] Remember, Hoess could activate humane concerns while at home and place them in a dormant state while at the Auschwitz camp. In the camp that "dormancy" so severely removed his humane concerns from activation that most observers would be readily convinced that Hoess has no humane concerns in his makeup.

THE COMPELLING POWER OF IMMEDIACY AND EXTRICATING ONESELF FROM TAKING PART IN EVIL

At My Lai an American soldier shot himself in the leg so that he no longer would need to participate in the killings. At Auschwitz a newly arrived SS officer was shocked to discover what was going on. He immediately requested to be transferred out of Auschwitz. The request was granted, and he was not penalized for making the request.

These two were exceptions. The majority of soldiers at My Lai did not try to get out of taking part in the killings. Instead, they became thoroughly immersed and increasingly zealous in the course of that morning's actions. And the majority of SS men did not try to leave Auschwitz.

Dr. Kremer, after first grumbling about the horrors of Auschwitz, became used to them and participated unreservedly. Hoess, too, had early moments of unease about the horrors he was creating and implementing, but he continued the horrors. And what is more, he did so with ever-growing and awesome zeal.

The "ordinary people" whom Stanley Milgram recruited for his experiments also began by grumbling about being asked to inflict pain on innocent people. But they soon went along with instructions and gradually became entirely immersed in what they believed were actions that inflicted increasing hurt on innocent people.

The lesson seems to be that one can extricate oneself from a horrendous situation by acting immediately, while one's "outside" perspective is still intact. However, once having begun to participate in horrendous activities, these activities, and the context in which they are being carried out, can become terribly compelling. One's "outside" perspective can be shunted aside in favor of a very localized and very immediate interpretation of the world. Moral myopia prevails. This should remind us of the gambler who tells himself "I need just one more round, then I'll give it up and go straight," the drug addict who needs just one more fix and will then give it up, and the high-flying junk-bond broker of the 1980s who needed to make just a few more million dollars before turning to a life of decency.

It should also remind us of the infantry soldier engaged in hand-to-hand killing in the First World War and in the American Civil War where, in face-to-face confrontation on many a single day, thousands of men hacked or shot each other to death; where relatives occasionally found each other on opposing sides, hacking away at each other; where, as in most wars, innocent people kill innocent people; and where, in the heat of battle, the individual soldier finds it unthinkable to do anything other than continue to slaughter human beings whom someone had designated as his enemies. (I have emphasized the First World War and the American Civil War, rather than more recent wars among modern nations because, in these more recent wars, much—but not all— of the killing is done more and more impersonally, by the use of machine technology and at long range. Of course in both kinds of wars the dead are just as dead. But the personal awareness of participating in slaughter is different.)

In many a situation, once outside perspectives are eliminated, one is attuned only to the immediacy in which one now exists. This immediacy, even when it centers on killing, can generate its own momentum. It can become totally compelling. Recall the Marine general's statement: "What do soldiers fight for?... They fight for their buddies." Translated, why do soldiers kill?... They kill for their buddies, for those in their immediate combat unit.

And the compelling power of immediate circumstances can have long-term addictive impact. Old soldiers recall and relive dangerous battles in periodic celebrations. Even former enemies, such as British and German pilots who had fought each other during the Second World War, get together for reunions to celebrate their past battle encounters. And note, the Auschwitz guards who, twenty years after having committed their deeds, were still able to beam with joy when reminded of their deeds. They were able to relive some of the excitement they had experienced in the immediate moment when they were so creatively producing evil.

A very different long-term impact is exemplified by veterans suffering from Posttraumatic Stress Disorder. Horrifying specifics of past immediacies continue to haunt these former soldiers. They remain riders to their present life

The lesson, let me repeat, is that extricating oneself from participating in evil actions is most feasible if one acts right away upon recognizing the situation. After that, after actually participating in evil, it becomes increasingly difficult to do so. In traditional psychological language, one finds ways to rationalize, to justify, one's participation in evil once one has begun to take part in it. In terms of behavior packages and riders, one accepts a rider that so organizes the components of one's behavior package that humane concerns are relegated to the background. It takes some perverse courage to reject the prevailing rider from the immediate circumstances in which one finds oneself, adopt a different rider, and thereby assert an alternative frame of reference.

The positive side is that even when one takes part in evil, one's humane inclinations may not be obliterated; they may merely have been shunted aside. If so, they can be retrieved. But this may take some harsh actions, such as shooting oneself in the leg, as the American soldier did at My Lai, or long-term psychotherapy to work on the retrieval of one's humanity.

ANOTHER LOOK AT THE FIVE PARADOXES: SOME ANSWERS, SOME NEW QUESTIONS, SOME HOPE.

The book began by citing five paradoxes that either help to create evil or prevent us from coming to grips with understanding evil. Now, to illustrate that we have choices that can lead to turning away from evil, let us return to these paradoxes. But this time the emphasis is on positive features inherent in the five paradoxes, those leading toward avoidance of evil.

This new perspective will suggest answers to some old questions but will, in turn, raise new questions that have to be addressed in the future. By reading this book you have joined the venture to gain mastery over evil. Raising new questions is part of that venture. We need not fear new questions. Progress consists of answering one set of questions with a better set of questions. In this spirit I am nearing the end of the book with some new questions. I hope the book has said enough to enlist you in the added venture—the adventure—of answering these new questions. Meanwhile, the new questions constitute a new level of understanding. And when it comes to evil, that new level of understanding can, at long last, lead us to some real mastery over evil.

Paradox 1. Very Ordinary Persons May Make Very
Extraordinary Contributions to Evil

Answer: *ordinary persons can also subvert evil, and bureaucrats can turn away from serving evil bureaucracies.* National leaders who harbor grandly murderous dreams, such as the Hitlers and Stalins of this century, cannot work out the detailed tactics and strategies to implement their own dreams. When Hitler tried to devise detailed tactics and strategy himself, as he occasionally did in military measures against Russia and Britain, it resulted in utter failure for the German military machine. Most of the time leaders rely on organizations, and the full gamut of people who work in them, from high-level administrators to low-level functionaries, to devise and implement the tactics and strategies to implement their dreams. Stated differently, large organizations are a modern society's machinery for reaching goals, and it takes input from many people to operate this machinery. This machinery, and the people who operate it, sometimes sabotage the leader's dreams. But we are not clear when this is apt to happen.

Benito Mussolini, dictator of Italy in the 1920s and 1930s, dreamed of having an awesomely efficient army with which to create a modern Italian empire. He did create what he believed to be such an army. As long as this army fought vastly outnumbered, undisciplined, underequipped opponents, it did well. However, against opponents who had equipment and personnel roughly comparable to itself it performed miserably. Military efficiency was not implemented. It is not clear exactly how the Italian military organization resisted their leader's dreams, but resist them they did. Perhaps there exists a pervasive rider to the behavior of modern Italians that says: "We long ago lost our Roman Empire, but we have gained the wisdom to live without it; no Mussolini or Hitler is going to drag us back into a life of militarism and obedience to authoritarian control." (Such assertiveness may also have been at work when Italians refused to go along with German pressure to persecute Italian Jews.)

Why did not the German army subvert the grandiose dreams of Hitler, as the Italian army subverted Mussolini? Under which circumstances will persons who serve in bureaucratic organizations donate their energy, their imagination, their skills to the cause of evil? Under which circumstances will they balk at evil? Subvert evil?

A ray of hope emanates from the fact that bureaucratic skills are transferable. Bureaucrats are rarely permanently attached to a particular ideology. Although bureaucrats, such as Hoess, will use an ideology to justify their deeds within one bureaucracy, they are also capable to switching ideologies, particularly when they leave one bureaucracy and join another.

The specialty of bureaucrats is administration. They carry out their administrative activities while also pursuing their personal career, whose advancement may be linked to the survival of the organization in which they work. To pursue their careers they are prepared to adapt their daily activities and their loyalties. For example, toward the end of the Second World War, Himmler, the head of the SS, recognized that Germany was losing the war. He adapted by trying to end the exterminations and conceal the traces of what had been done. This went far beyond a criminal not wanting to be found out, of hiding the evidence so that, if he were caught, he might be spared punishment. There is indication that Himmler was trying to curry the Allies' favor so that he might continue to serve as a high-level bureaucrat for the soon-to-be-victorious Allied powers. Given Himmler's history of unparalleled contribution to Nazi evil, his plan may seem weird, to put it mildly. But his plan was entirely in character for a professional bureaucrat! If your career does not work out in one organization, you join another. You will then apply your administrative skills to whatever objectives that new organization pursues.

In the modern world, much hope lies in the fact that bureaucratic skills are very transferable and bureaucrats can donate their career to a new cause without changing many of their daily habits. For example, the American Secretary of Defense during the Reagan administration, Caspar Weinberger, was very successful in persuading the United States Congress that the military establishment required ever-more funds for ever-more killing power. He effectively championed this as a major national priority, under a rider of the Reagan administration, one of its major themes, that there was need for a stronger military defense. Some years earlier this same civil servant presided over the Department of Health and Welfare. In that capacity he successfully persuaded the Congress to provide funds for programs to foster human health. There is hope here. This Secretary of Defense, who staunchly advocated preparedness for war, was not a permanent, blood-curdling militarist. He was merely an effective and loyal bureaucrat, who contributed his administrative skills to a variety of policies. After serving as Secretary of Defense he may again turn his skills to peaceful pursuits.

Given the flexibility of bureaucrats, and given their limited commitment to any particular ideology (as even Hoess showed us), how can one wean bureaucrats away from active participation in outright evil by the bureaucracy in which they currently work?

Paradox 2. Persons Most Affected by Horrendous Deeds May Unwittingly Stand in the Way of Understanding the Causes of These Deeds

They do so by emphasizing the singularity, the uniqueness, of the horrors they have experienced.

Answer: *those who seek to discover universal behavior principles, through scientific analyses of "singular" horrors, seek to discover ways to lessen or prevent singular horrors in the future. And those who emphasize the singularity of a horror, such as the Holocaust, also touch on its universality.*

The book has discussed how survivors of the Holocaust are, necessarily and understandably, gripped by the uniqueness of the Holocaust. To be sure this can lead to some antagonism toward anyone who would compare the Holocaust to other human horrors. Yet when the uniqueness of the Holocaust is emphasized to the fullest, as in the work of Elie Wiesel, it can create a universality of its own. Who, upon listening to Wiesel, has not felt that he speaks not just for Jews, and not just for Holocaust victims, but for all humans who suffer? His words are about one awesome occurrence, but his message is about humanity. The same held true for Gandhi, speaking of the suffering of Indians, and for Martin Luther King, Jr., speaking of the suffering of American Blacks. Theirs is the approach of the humanist, the poet, the novelist, the playwright. Theirs is the approach of the leader, the prophet, the visionary. Finally, theirs is the approach of the engaged human being, the person for whom horrendous deeds are a personal call to action, the Raoul Wallenbergs of the world. But these persons are not likely to so distance themselves from the horrors that they can pursue the scientific challenge of discovering the causes of the horrors. Yet theirs is a noble quest. No one can dispute its moral force, precisely because of its touch of universality.

Nonetheless, this book has emphasized the scientific effort toward understanding evil. The approach of the scientist is not a substitute for that of the humanist, the leader, or the engaged human being. Rather, it adds another dimension, teaching us more accurately how evil is produced. From this the scientist may eventually create reliable ways of predicting and preventing further horrendous occurrences or, failing that, of counteracting horrors before they reach their most malignant state.

It is not enough to remember and teach about horrors. Imploring people not to forget is no guarantee that past horrors will not be repeated. For instance, given the human capacity for creating new riders, past horrors can be reinterpreted and become enticing models that some people will want to emulate by repeating the horrors. Mourning and massive commemorations confer little or no immunity against future social horrors. Teaching about horrors relies heavily on the assumption that people will experience such revulsion that they will, under no circumstances, engage in such horrors, that revulsion will serve as a vaccine against committing horrors. Yet one thing we learn from the life of Hoess is that a person can have a real sense of revulsion about murderous activities, yet engage in them with alacrity and fervor.

In the past, despite the repeated arousal of abhorrence about horrendous evil, we were abysmally ignorant of why evil happened and how to prevent it in the future. All along large-scale evil continued to be perpetrated. Since the Holocaust, during the Second World War, there have been massive killings in Cambodia, Biafra, Afghanistan, Iran and Iraq, to mention just a few of "at least forty-four sustained episodes of mass murder against ethnic and political minorities,"[5] resulting in several million deaths and misery for many more. The small country of Cambodia saw about 1.5 million of its people killed in the 1970s. One thing most of these horrors have in common, and in common with previous horrors, is that they were not predicted. Great horrors continually catch people by surprise. Another thing they have in common is that knowledge of horrors committed in the past provided no immunity against new horrors. There is no substitute for far more dispassionate knowledge about the causes and dynamics of the horrors.

We can achieve far more effective knowledge about the ways in which evil is produced. We can do so if we eliminate some of our mental blinders. For example, when paying attention to particular horrors, we must not confuse accumulating more and more information with creating effective knowledge. A huge amount of information already exists about major horrors, such as the Holocaust; libraries and archives are filled with records and descriptions of what happened and more information continues to accumulate. Collecting such information is indeed important. But even more important is how the information is analyzed—where one does not assume that facts speak for themselves. While there is a surfeit of information, there remains a shortage of effective knowledge.

Analyzing major horrors from the point of view that they are generated from within the range of ordinary people's ordinary behavior, as this book tries to do, offers the hope that we can move beyond remembering the past toward safeguarding the future, including prevention of additional "singular" horrors. Reconsidering the remaining paradoxes begins to address this issue.

Paradox 3. Horrendous Deeds May Be Performed While Persons Address Themselves to Fairly Innocuous, Immediate Problems

Answer: *concentration on immediacy does not necessarily lead to doing evil. Indeed, it can equally lead to a life of doing good deeds. Behavior can be redirected away from evil, using the same approach to immediate problems—focusing entirely on the immediacy—as can be used for the production of evil.* Recall the example of Raoul Wallenberg, who, concentrating on manipulating the immediate situation, subverted horrendous plans, even though it pitted him against a large bureaucracy. He thereby produced good on an extraordinary scale.

Psychologists who practice behavior modification concentrate on teaching individuals to cope with immediacy to wean them away from destructive activities and turn them toward constructive, wholesome living. The method often works because within every immediate situation there are choices to be made, and we can learn to make new choices. These choices, once made, accumulate. What we choose today will influence what we choose tomorrow. The acts of decision making in one's immediate situation may indeed obscure evil deeds, but there is nothing inevitable in this process. It can be interrupted and guided into new directions.

The interruption does not necessarily have to come from outside. I cited two examples: the American soldier who shot himself in the leg so that he no longer would have to take part in the My Lai horrors, and the SS officer, newly assigned to a concentration camp, who was so appalled by what he saw that he requested a reassignment. On the other hand, do not underestimate the momentum of an ongoing horrendous course of action. A helicopter pilot who observed the My Lai horrors from above repeatedly tried to interrupt the killings. He failed. This shows that the helicopter pilot—and the rest of us—do not yet have all the answers. Yet as we begin to recognize the option of shunting aside basic values in our immediate situation, we will become aware of the possibility of great evil through our own immediate activities. And, once aware of this possibility, we will be in a better position to avoid becoming contributors to evil.

Paradox 4. Evil May Be Flaunted by People Who Know Better

Answer: *even here no mysterious forces are at work, merely ordinary human behavior processes. We humans can take charge against evil, just as we can take charge in other realms of our lives.* The preceding pages have shown that persons who know the difference between good and evil may deliberately choose evil. These persons may not be mentally deranged persons, but very ordinary sorts of persons. And, to top it all, they may proudly show off their evil, flaunting it for all to see.

Evildoers use ordinary human behavior as their tools. (When I say *ordinary human behavior* I include making decisions; pursuing careers; reacting to other people; organizing our lives into compartments; using the freedom we have.) The ordinariness in the behavior of evildoers can give us hope.

First, *we can demystify evil.* No alien powers are at work in evil, merely human beings responding to the context in which they find themselves and making decisions on their own. This knowledge can empower us to take charge of our lives in realms of evil, just as we do in other realms.

Some persons hold onto the myth that compellingly "evil" forces are at work in human affairs. These people are apt to believe in attempts to find and excise the evil forces, just as surgeons attempt to find and excise cancers. The most well-intentioned and noble of these attempts are war crimes trials, such as those held at Nuremberg after the Second World War, which were an effort to cleanse Germany, and indeed the world, of the Nazi evil. The lawyers tried to hold outrageous criminals accountable for their actions. To some extent they succeeded, but to some extent they failed.

The Nuremberg trial lawyers made heroic efforts to demonstrate that they could identify thoroughly evil individuals and expose the full measure of their evil nature. But, alas, at the Nuremberg trials sat the pudgy, smiling Goering; some years later, at the Jerusalem trial, sat the pedantic, earnest Eichmann. Despite their horrendous deeds, both were revealed as individuals who retained much ordinariness. To be sure their *deeds* were morally outrageous beyond all measure. But these men sitting in the dock did not seem to personify an evil force. The more they talked about themselves, the more difficult it became to pinpoint an evil force at work. The more the lawyers tried to find a core of evil, the more these defendants looked maddeningly ordinary.[6]

For these reasons the Nuremberg trials, and the Eichmann trial later, left a bitter aftertaste about the capabilities of the legal profession. The law's efforts to cleanse the body politic fell short. Its implicit claim that it could find, expose, and excise evil turned out to be naive, if not arrogant. But let us not blame lawyers, who are sometimes cast in the role of society's shaman—sent out to find evil, hold it up for us to look at, and then destroy it for us. The bitter aftertaste should be attached to all of us who believe that evil is a separate and distinct entity. We need not continue to believe in this piece of witchcraft.[7]

Second, we must admit that, *under some circumstances, individuals will deliberately choose to do evil.* For example, a culture of cruelty can be highly attractive. It can offer an individual the opportunity to live creatively, and creative living touches on a profound human yearning. At times individuals may discover that acting cruelly is a way, perhaps the only way, they can be creative. They are then likely to embrace a culture of cruelty when some facilitating conditions exist in their immediate context. Also, a culture of cruelty can augment existing roles in a workplace, as it did for the guards at Auschwitz.

Third, returning to demystifying evil, by acknowledging that evil is at times embraced deliberately, as an attractive option, we are taking a step toward dispassionate knowledge of evil, and thereby showing that we have an option to *actively move away from debilitating mysticism.* This frees us to ask, Under which circumstances do people deliberately choose evil? In common parlance, we speak of people sometimes choosing the lesser of two evils when they must choose between options which are both unpleasant. But it seems that people sometimes deliberately choose the greatest evil. When do they do so? Sometimes they do so when a specific rider comes along and influences a wide range of behavior.

Paradox 5. Over Time Little May Change But, with a New Rider, Everything is Different

Answer: *riders need not be permanent. Tomorrow's rider may be very different from today's rider. New riders can be created deliberately.*

Consider: During the Second World War America viewed Japan as an enemy of the United States. This was the dominant rider to American actions toward the Japanese. The Japanese people were feared and distrusted to the extent that persons of Japanese ancestry, although born in the United States, were uprooted from their homes and sent to special internment camps. After the war a new rider emerged. Under it, for some forty years, Japan came to be seen as a friend of the United States. The Japanese people came to be trusted and esteemed. The American government, acting under a new rider, made plans for some financial restitution to the Japanese-Americans who had been interned.

From a long-term perspective an encouraging aspect of the change of riders is that, in the fury of raging hatred toward a particular group, good human qualities—such as generous, caring ways of relating to members of that group—may be suspended only temporarily, awaiting reactivation when a different rider prevails. Of course this is small comfort to the victims of persecution during an upsurge of hatred. It may even lead to serious misjudgment of the dangers one faces when a new rider first emerges and its full potency is not yet recognized. This happened in Germany. There, in the early years of the Nazis' voicing of virulent anti-Semitism, some Jews asked skeptically, "Are they going to kill all of us?" "Surely," they told themselves, "the Nazis cannot mean what they are saying. They cannot be that bad. The underlying goodness of the German people is bound to prevail." They underestimated the impact of the Nazi anti-Semitism as rider to the total range of behavior among the German people.

The encouraging side is that riders can change, and as a result, today's posture need not be tomorrow's posture. Today's rearrangement of yesterday's practices can be rearranged again tomorrow. Behavior postures toward other people are not permanent and rigid structures.[8]

However, knowing this should not make us complacent, particularly as the process can work both ways. When relations between any two categories of people are friendly and cooperative, then the hatred, fears, and prejudices between them may still remain alive, but exist in a dormant state within an existing package, temporarily suspended but subject to reactivation if a new rider prevails in the future. For instance, beneath the post-Second World War climate of America's positive sentiments toward the Japanese people lingered fears and prejudices about the Japanese people. These were reactivated as economic competition between the two countries accelerated in the 1990s, creating a new rider to American behavior toward the Japanese people. Comparably, the history of anti-Semitism is a history of periodic activation and deactivation of fears, prejudices, and hatred, each operating under the sponsorship of prevailing riders.

This pattern also counters yet another fondly held folk belief. We believe that hatred, fears, and prejudices can be fully eradicated—particularly through appropriate education, appropriate confrontation of issues, appropriate "getting to know you" interactions between people who have a history of enmity. In actuality history teaches us that hatred, fears, and prejudices between categories of people sometimes reemerge after long periods of time, when it was thought that they had been completely eradicated. For example, the Jews of Germany were the most assimilated of Jews. Many of them believed that, above all in Germany, anti-Semitism was largely eradicated. Yet precisely there, in Germany, the most malignant form of anti-Semitism erupted in the twentieth century. Remember, too, the very long-standing hostilities between Protestants and Catholics of Europe that have survived periods of amiable relations between these religions. And remember, too, the recalcitrance of hatred between Hindus and Moslems on the Indian subcontinent.

I do not claim that hatred, fears, and prejudices can never be fully and permanently eradicated. I am saying, merely, that our folk belief in their eradication does not take into account their persistence and resilience. It does not take into account the fact that the raw material for active hatred may exist in *dormant* form among the components of a package long after it seems to have been eradicated because its surface manifestations have disappeared.

This is not a call for pessimism. I am not saying that we should give up the quest for hate-free societies and a hate-free world. But we can become more effective, in pursuing such an objective, when we become realistic about the workings of packages and riders. This includes recognizing that long after the surface manifestations of hatred have disappeared, deep hatred, fears, and prejudices between social groups may linger on; these can erupt again when new riders emerge to rearrange the existing components of a package.

Riders are sometimes most conspicuous when there are abrupt social changes and reorganization of priorities is demanded. Here the riders may be very public and very explicit. They may underwrite profound changes, including some that move toward evil.

Let us consider this: Japan's raid on Pearl Harbor initiated America's entry into the Second World War. It also created a dramatic new rider. Before Pearl Harbor, America had generally favored the Allied powers—Britain, France and Russia—in their fight against Germany. The U.S. government had sent them considerable economic and military aid. But actually joining the fighting was viewed with ambivalence. There were also voices on behalf of the German side, including open sympathizers with Nazi anti-Semitism. Followers of Father Coughlin's pro-German and anti-Semitic crusade of the 1920s and 1930s were still very much alive.

All this changed with the raid on Pearl Harbor by Germany's ally, Japan. Support for Nazism was suddenly utterly discredited. The new dominant rider, for Americans, was that America was at war with Germany and Japan. It accepted no compromise. All cooperation with Germany or Japan was regarded as treason. America was defined to be in a mortal fight. This required complete national unity and solidarity. In most ways Americans were still the Americans of old, yet they now operated under new priorities that created stark changes.

In retrospect, some actions taken, such as the internment of Japanese-Americans, were evil choices. But other actions, also derived from the new rider, were not evil at all. In other words, riders are not inherently evil. They are simply ordinary mechanisms in our social existence. As such they can lend themselves to doing good and to doing evil. But mostly a new rider can authorize drastic changes in priorities. The danger is that these drastic changes can easily trample upon freedom and humane concerns that had evolved over long periods of give-and-take in human communal living.

How can one ensure that drastic changes authorized by a new rider will not open the floodgates to evil? What will alert us when a new rider asks us to cross a threshold between humane and evil behavior? It would be useful to develop indicators of a threshold being crossed. The participants in the Milgram experiment probably had no such indicators in their personal repertoire; hence their readiness to do evil. Neither did the participants in the My Lai action; hence their readiness to do evil.

Remember, riders often operate by rearranging the priorities of our lives rather than substituting entirely new ways of living. This makes us vulnerable to being seduced by new riders. But it also means that after one rider has served to shunt aside humane and moral practices, another rider can be created to retrieve and re-mobilize these practices, and thus help us retreat from manufacturing evil.

THE LARGER PICTURE

Modernism and the Potentials for Evil

As the twentieth century comes to an end we are increasingly disenchanted with the social philosophy of Modernism. We are finally learning some lessons about the shortcomings of Modernism. But there is one lesson we have still not learned: recognizing ways in which Modernism contains potentials for evil. This book tries to bring the potentials for evil into focus. As this focus becomes clearer we may achieve more realistic mastery over evil. Perhaps the twenty-first century will see it happen.

The first half of the twentieth century saw great enchantment with Modernism. We seemed to have entered an era where the fruits of science and the systematic use of reason appeared to offer enormous blessings—better health, longer life, more material abundance for an ever-larger portion of the world's people. (Recall Bertrand Russell's optimism about the glorious benefits to be derived from the increasing use of reason.) There seemed to be an evolutionary trend in human social affairs, moving us toward ever-greater societal improvement, as the nineteenth century evolutionists had promised us by way of the biological sciences.

It has not worked out this way. In the second half of the twentieth century disenchantment with Modernism has set in. We have had to learn that the modern nation-state, with its monopoly on the "legitimate" use of violence, is under very few moral constraints.[9] As a result, we have seen monstrous uses of violence by the modern nation-state, sometimes directed against its own citizens, sometimes directed against external enemies. To be sure there have been efforts at introducing some moral sanity into the political realm—there was the League of Nations, trying to promote international cooperation after the First World War; there were the World Federalists, trying to create a single world government after the Second World War; and last, and still trying to promote world peace, there is the United Nations organization, which has recently shown some renewed signs of life. None of these efforts at moral sanity in the political realm have prevented the litany of political horrors of our time. (Perhaps, without these efforts there would have been even more political horrors. Perhaps.)

It is not only in the political realm that Modernism has failed us. Other major sectors of our modern social existence—modern economics, modern law, and modern science—have all failed to curb evil. Indeed, every one has been a partner in evil.

Modern economic activity, with its veneration of the profit motive, operates with moral blinders so frequently, so typically, that no elaboration is needed. The Nazis did not need to twist many arms to get major German business firms to collaborate in the Holocaust. To this day, in many countries, in many parts of the globe, the manufacture of weapons of destruction is regarded as perfectly good economics.

Modern law showed itself a willing and eager partner to creating and implementing Hitler's horrors (just as it helped to implement Stalin's horrors in the Soviet Union). And the law in other countries, in other times, up to the present, usually operates in lock-step with whatever social climate prevails. Modern law, just like modern medicine and modern religion, has rarely stood in the forefront against modern evil, especially when it encounters evil on the grandest scale. Only when it encounters safely agreed-upon evil, when it comes to cracking down on the little crook, law joins us in trumpeting our righteous indignation. But it must be mentioned that the law's efforts in the American Civil Rights Movement stands as a noble exception. Here the law did indeed address grand-scale evil. But there are not many instances of the law exercising moral leadership of such magnitude. (And, in the Civil Rights Movement much of the leadership and energy came from the political and religious sectors of American life, in addition to the legal sector.)

Science seemed to epitomize the unfettered use of the modernized human mind to create a better world. It did produce a range of knowledge that has given us a level of power we could not have imagined even a half-century ago. It has given us magnificent products and technology. But it has also given us atomic weapons and other instruments of horror. Perhaps even more important, it has given us a posture, a way of addressing the world, that is methodically effective while, at the same time, it is so morally unconstrained that the manufacture of great evil is well within its purview. There are serious scholars who say that "the scientific mode of thought and the methodology attached to it were intrinsic to the mass killings [that took place during the Holocaust]...the mentality of modern science is what made the Holocaust possible..."[10]

Despite its possible contribution to social horrors, I do not believe that we should give up on science. Indeed, I believe that science—so uniquely suited to discovering truth in nature, but not at all suited to discovering moral guidelines—is perhaps our only hope of eventually getting effective control over evil. It will do so if we allow science to do what it does best—to be dispassionate, creative and committed to truth—in order to address the problem of how evil is actually produced. Science cannot make moral decisions for us; science does not automatically eliminate the beguilings of evil. But science can clarify for us how these beguilings operate. It can thereby show us where and when, in response to the beguilings of evil, we must make moral decisions, and which moral decisions must be made, and what the consequences are of not making moral decisions.

Our modern world contains distinctive moral compromises and, therefrom, potentials for evil. Let us consider just those derived from the political arrangements designed to safeguard nationhood. These arrangements incorporate moral compromises that justified, to Germans in the early 1940s, their country's conducting a Holocaust on a portion of its citizens and, to Germany's enemies of that period, conducting saturation fire-bombing air raids on enemy cities (which, during the Second World War, probably caused more civilian casualties than the atomic bomb raids). Both sets of mass killings were carried out under the umbrella of the moral compromises built into modern nationalism. That modern nationalism is part of the fabric of the modern social order. Within that fabric, the societal arrangements under which we live out our lives, there exist potentials for evildoing. And potentials for evildoing tend to be translated into actual evildoing. They do so through the packaging of programs and the impact of riders upon the behavior of individuals in their everyday life. (Recall the impact of the violation-of-Germans'-rightful-grandeur rider upon the behavior of individuals.)

Yet this is not the whole story. The book you have just read suggests that actual evildoing, itself, has distinctive characteristics that are part of the fabric of our social order and of our personal lives as members of our society. In our modern world evildoing can provide us career opportunities. Evildoing can solve problems for us. And, what is more, we usually do not need to invent and fight for our own personal brand of evil. Often the context in which we find ourselves supplies and nurtures evil for us.

Modern society includes potentials for long-term evildoing, with opportunity for developing personal careers around evildoing—such as those that actually took place in the Auschwitz culture of cruelty and the culture of greed in America in the 1980s. It also includes potentials for short-term evildoing, such as the My Lai events that gave soldiers relief from frustration. Short-term evil also includes certain deliberate actions during the 1988 American presidential campaign.

Stated differently, our modern world contains much potential for evildoing. The examples of actual evildoing just cited are instances of the translation of these potentials into practical realities. More such translations can be expected to happen—if we do not address the problem of evil as a practical issue arising in modern communal living.

What the Culture of Cruelty Teaches Us

There are phenomena, such as human beings finding joy in acting cruelly toward other human beings, which most sane people regard as totally abhorrent. Yet these phenomena can erupt in our world on the basis of entirely natural attributes within ourselves.

And these phenomena are no more the result of an evil nature within ourselves—of a cruel streak in us—than is the eruption of cancer in our bodies the result of a cancerous nature in ourselves. Both are aberrations that utilize our existing makeup—the same makeup that can be utilized for doing wholesome, constructive and loving things.

To say that evildoing is a naturally occurring activity in human societies is not to condone evildoing, any more than saying that cancer in our bodies must be condoned because it is a naturally occurring process.

In practice, how does it look when our makeup is utilized so that we do cruel things deliberately and joyfully? Two examples— the stabilized culture of cruelty at Auschwitz and the short-lived culture of cruelty at My Lai—were used to illustrate how such phenomena can actually look. Of course these are not the only instances of deliberate and joyfully enacted cruelty on a large scale.[11] But they do start us out on realistic investigation of the processes whereby we do evil joyfully, using our existing makeup.

What About the Role of Bureaucracies in Modern Evil?

It has long been recognized that the Nazis used bureaucratic organizations to help implement the mass production of death. In many ways the concentration camps were run like modern factories. And thanks to the writings of the sociologist Max Weber it has long been recognized, too, that bureaucracies harness the expertise of professionals; in bureaucracies people are utilized and rewarded for their technical knowledge.

What has not been recognized sufficiently is that bureaucracies also offer scope and rewards for personal creativity and inventiveness, thereby creating a measure of individuality for the individual functionary. In the concentration camps this emerged around the core mission of the camps, the manufacture of murderous cruelty. One's personal creativity was apt to be demonstrated in one's invention of new ways to be cruel.

There is a wider issue here. In our modern world, work has lost much of its dignity. There is little esteem for craftsmanship, for satisfaction in doing one's work well, for giving one's work a personal tinge, for producing a product that will permanently display the personal artistry of the individual who made it. It seems to me that the trial of SS guards demonstrated, aside from the malignancy and viciousness of their behavior, a desperate hunger for doing something creative, and being recognized for it. Surely the quest for finding some activity in life where one can be creative touches on something deep in us. Most of us, most of the time, fail to find it. But the quest continues, as traditional American factory workers have shown us: although stuck in highly routine tasks they often found ways to introduce a measure of personal creativity.

What About Personal Careers and the Beguilings of Evil?

In our modern world, the very fiber of much of personal life centers around one's career. And yet nowadays careers are increasingly unplannable, unpredictable and, yes, uncertain.

From Dr. Doe we saw that careers almost certainly involve compromises. We do things we do not really want to do, even when we are humane individuals and want to produce a service that has genuine value.

From Dr. Kremer we saw that compromises can lead to horrendous consequences and contribute to great evil. And the threshold between a minor, nebulous compromise and a major, morally dangerous compromise is usually not clearly marked.

Our personal careers—be it one's occupational career, one's marital career, one's communal career, or even, one's career in religiosity—are typically undertaken with very little guidance (guidance counselors notwithstanding). Along the way, in the course of our careers, we have to take risks, because if we do not take risks we are, for all practical purposes, entirely dead.

The decisions we make, though often small and localized, are apt to have cumulative consequences we cannot predict. And, as

Hoess teaches us, the consequences of small, localized decisions may indeed be the journey to horrendous evil. One of the beguilings of evil consists of not showing its full face to us at any one time; we glimpse only small parts, parts we think we can keep under control.

Zealots and Their Unwitting Partners

We are well warned about zealots—the True Believers, the fanatics, the Hitlers—who come our way.

This book warns us about an entirely different sort of person: the serious pragmatist; the earnest, pedantic individual; the Hoesses, the Stangls, the Eichmanns. These, too, can be terribly dangerous. They can be unwitting partners in zealotry, contributing mightily to evil by applying their inverted imagination, their stunted autonomy, to implementing the grandiose dreams of demented leaders.

Lifting Oneself by the Bootstraps—Inventing the Tools to Understand Evildoing in Our Midst:

Although some scientists, such as Adorno, Milgram, Kelman and Hamilton (to name just a few of many) have attempted to find ways to understand evil behavior, we still have a long distance to go before we really understand the occurrence of horrendous levels of evil in our own time. With these scientists I share the conviction that we are dealing with phenomena that can be known and, therefore, eventually curbed, rather than dealing with mysterious, basically unknowable forces that are essentially beyond us or consist of a convergence of historical circumstances entirely unique to each event. And with them I operate from the premise that we must create the scientific tools for understanding how evil is produced—facts do *not* speak for themselves—and (I think they might agree) that we still do not have an adequate science for doing so. We must create the science as we go along—lift ourselves by our own bootstraps.

To create that science requires a delicate balancing act. One must be immersed in the facts, in thoroughly knowing actual evil deeds. Yet one must stand back and, as a dispassionate outsider, devise ways of dissecting the facts in ways that make them understood in an effective way. This second facet requires inventiveness. One must create *constructs*, ways of thinking about human behavior, that will serve as tools.

This book exposes such a balancing act, describing some evil events and activities and, at the same time, devising constructs to help understand them. The constructs used—*incremental* decision making, *packages*, *riders*, and forms of *autonomy*—are intended to help understand how one participates in the social circumstances in which one finds oneself and how these social circumstances have a dynamic reality of their own. This is not a complete new social psychology, a fully worked-out scientific system about human social behavior; it is merely a beginning. If this beginning succeeds in increasing our powers of explanation—and control—over evil then it will serve a good purpose. If this beginning adds to our understanding of ordinary human behavior, it will give us the extra bonus of extracting something wholesome from the killing fields we know as extraordinary evil. If this beginning encourages us to continue the quest to master evil, we may accomplish something worthwhile for the world of our children.

*   *   *

Ordinary sorts of people, using ordinary behavior, have contributed to extraordinary evil, creating major horrors. As we understand more accurately how the ordinary can be harnessed for doing evil, we make progress toward a new freedom: the freedom to stop manufacturing extraordinary evil. There is hope.

NOTES

INTRODUCTION: FROM THE ORDINARY TO THE EXTRAORDINARY

1. A notable exception was Helen Fein's book, *Accounting for Genocide: National Responses and Jewish Victimization During the Holocaust* (Chicago: University of Chicago Press, 1979). Fein compared the fate of Jews in the different countries occupied by the Germans in the Hitler era. By focusing on the different ways in which Jews were integrated into their respective countries she was able to come to striking conclusions about the likelihood of Jews surviving in any one country.

Zygmunt Bauman, also a sociologist, notes that, compared to historians' very active work on the Holocaust, the Holocaust work of sociologists "looks more like a collective exercise in forgetting and eye-closing." Zygmunt Bauman, *Modernity and the Holocaust* (Ithaca, N.Y.: Cornell University Press, 1989), pp. 8–9.

2. Theodore Adorno, E. Frenkel-Brunswik, D. J. Levinson, and R. N. Sanford, *The Authoritarian Personality* (New York: Harper and Row, 1950).

3. Stanley Milgram, *Obedience to Authority: An Experimental View* (New York: Harper and Row, 1974). For a systematic survey study of the moral impact of obedience, see Herbert C. Kelman and V. Lee Hamilton, *Crimes of Obedience: Toward a Social Psychology of Authority and Responsibilty* (New Haven, Conn.: Yale University Press, 1989).

4. Milgram comes very close to this point of view. The very last statement in his book is "the social psychology of this century reveals a major lesson: often it is not so much the kind of person a man is as the kind of situation in which he finds himself that determines how he will act." Ibid., p. 205.

Milgram himself notes what I am calling a beguiling process: once the individual has begun to do evil, the individual is apt to continue doing evil, rather than "say to himself. 'Everything I have done to this point is bad, and now I acknowledge it by breaking off.'" Ibid., p. 149.

5. Hannah Arendt, *Eichmann in Jerusalem: A Report on the Banality of Evil* (New York: Penguin Books, 1964).

6. Commandant Hoess was chosen not only because of his unique role as chief of Auschwitz during its most horrific period. He was chosen also because his autobiography, written while he was awaiting his execution, contradicts so many of our commonsense notions about the nature of evil, forcing us either to dismiss it out of hand, or to confront evildoing in a new way. This book attempts to take that second course. The story of Hoess is not a comprehensive study of concentration camp chiefs. A really comprehensive study of concentration camp chiefs was undertaken by Tom Segev, and reported in his book, *Soldiers of Evil: The Commandants of the Nazi Concentration Camps* (New York: McGraw-Hill, 1987). In the 1970s Segev interviewed three surviving concentration camp commandants, as well as relatives of several others. He also examined a large number of documents produced in the course of concentration camp administration.

Many of Segev's findings about concentration camp commandants parallel those of Hoess, to be reported here. But his analysis differs. His study is focused on comparing different individuals' careers. His guiding questions are, What were their motives? And, how could they have done what they did? The answer, he suggests, lies in their fanatical adherence to Nazi ideology. In this book I suggest how apparently "fanatical adherence" might evolve in the careers of fairly ordinary people, using ordinary—nonfanatical—behavior.

CHAPTER 1. CONFRONTING EVIL AND ITS PARADOXES

1. James R. Newman, *The World of Mathematics*, vol. 1 (New York: Simon and Schuster, 1956), pp. 370–380.

2. Hannah Arendt, *Eichmann in Jerusalem: A Report on the Banality of Evil*.

3. Ibid., p. 25.

4. Ibid., p. 25.

5. Ibid., p. 276.

6. The anger at Arendt was also based on another theme in her work, that the victims contributed to their own demise—her claim that, for example, were it not for the cooperation of Jewish leaders in rounding up fellow-Jews, the Nazis could not have succeeded in rounding up so many. I am not at all sure that the Jewish leaders deserve this blame.

But here, too, Arendt touches on an issue one cannot ignore: ordinary people's *cooperation* with evil enterprises.

7. If the route to evil is "ordinary" people engaged in "ordinary" behavior, there is a harsh possibility that every one of us could travel that route. After all, we are all ordinary. (Cf. Hans Askenasy's book title, *Are We All Nazis?* [Secaucus, N.J.: Lyle Stuart, 1978].) Passionate rejection of this possibility may well be one, among several reasons behind the reactions against Arendt's insight into the banality of Eichmann.

8. So believes Emil Fackenheim, a leading Jewish theologian and philosopher. He claims that Auschwitz sends this message to Jews: do not give Hitler a posthumous victory by giving up on the Jewish religion. See, *God's Presence in History* (New York: New York University Press, 1970).

9. I. L. Horowitz, *Taking Lives: Genocide and State Power* (New Brunswick, N.J.: Transaction Books, 1980), pp. 75, 87.

10. Milgram, *Obedience to Authority.*

11. Richard Hammer, *The Court-Martial of Lt. Calley* (New York: Coward, McCann, Geoghegan, 1971), pp. 269–270.

12. I was reminded of this passage by K. Seeskin's "The Reality of Radical Evil" in *Judaism* (Fall 1980). From Fyodor Dostoevski, *The Brothers Karamazov* (New York: New American Library, Signet Edition, 1960), pp. 219–220.

13. Ibid., p. 220.

14. Seeskin, "The Reality of Radical Evil," p. 445.

15. Richard Cavendish, *The Power of Evil in Western Religion, Magic and Folk Belief* (New York: Putnam, 1975), p. 77.

16. Ibid., p. 78.

17. Ibid., p. 78.

CHAPTER 2. BEHAVIOR MECHANISMS AT WORK

1. These numbers include killings during the Chinese Revolution, in 1911, and the Civil War that began in 1927 and ended in 1947, the government-directed mass executions in 1951, and the Sino-Japanese war of 1937–1945. Gil Eliot, *Twentieth Century Book of the Dead* (New York: Charles Scribner's Sons, 1972), Chapter 4.

2. Arthur Koestler, *Janus* (New York: Vintage Books, 1979), p. 77.

3. A similar way of looking at the Nazi package of values is that it was a full-fledged "ethic"—a system of beliefs that is internally consistent, that defines what is good and what is evil, and that has been grafted onto past German values but has substituted new "enemies" and "evils" for old ones. This viewpoint is developed by Peter J. Haas, in *Morality after Auschwitz: The Radical Challenge of the Nazi Ethic* (Philadelphia: Fortress Press, 1988). Haas states that "Nazi doctors, lawyers, theologians, teachers, camp commandants, and railway personnel did their jobs with dedication, determination, and professionalism that indicates that they found value in what they were doing" (page 1). They acted within a system of belief that was a repackaged version of previous German value packages.

I am convinced that the Nazi ethic, as Haas describes it, was indeed a major factor in producing the Holocaust evil. Here, I point to the ways in which human behavior, in its ordinariness, contributed to implementing that demented dream Haas describes as the Nazi ethic.

4. Before I seem too smug and self-righteous, I am well aware of an awkward question: Had I not been Jewish and left the village, would I have acted differently from the rest of the villagers? Probably not.

CHAPTER 3. SOME FACES OF EVIL

1. Dr. Doe was one of a series of physicians whose way of practicing medicine I observed in some depth during a previous study. He was not chosen statistically; I do not know how representative he is of the medical profession. I cite him here because he demonstrates a way of combining research-mindedness with a commitment to safeguarding the dignity of patients. See, Fred E. Katz, *Autonomy and Organization: The Limits of Social Control* (New York: Random House, 1968).

2. It does, however, require a commitment to a total package, within which there is an evil component.

3. The diary is translated and reprinted in Jadwiga Bezwinska and Danuta Czech, eds., *KL Auschwitz Seen by the SS: Hoess, Broad, Kremer*, 2d ed. (Oswiecimiu: Publications of the Panstwowe Muzeum, 1978).

4. Ibid., p. 207.

5. Ibid., p. 211.

6. Ibid., p. 211.

7. Ibid., p. 212.

8. Ibid., p. 214.

9. Ibid., p. 215.

10. Ibid., pp. 215–216.

11. Ibid., p. 218.

12. Ibid., p. 220.

13. Nowadays organ transplants make use of human tissue for entirely benign purposes. In Kremer's situation humans were deliberately killed to donate their "living fresh" organs.

14. *KL Auschwitz*, p. 220.

15. I have concentrated on the ways in which this physician linked up with an evil course of action. For another approach to physicians taking part in the Nazi program, with emphasis on physicians' possible pathology, see Robert J. Lifton, "The Medicalization of Killing," *Psychiatry* (Fall 1982) and *The Nazi Doctors: Medical Killing and the Psychology of Genocide* (New York: Basic Books, 1986).

16. Richard Rubenstein, *After Auschwitz* (Indianapolis: Bobbs-Merrill, 1975), p. 60.

17. Robert Conquest, *Harvest of Sorrow: Collectivization and the Terror of Famine* (New York: Oxford University Press, 1986), p. 343.

18. Much of what follows uses information that Hoess himself provided. During his time in prison, before he was executed in April 1947, he wrote a very detailed autobiography. It is published as, Rudolf Hoess, *Commandant of Auschwitz* trans. C. Fitz-Gibbon (New York: World Publishing Company, 1959). The book gives every indication of being an honest statement of how Hoess remembered his life.

19. If we believe that Hoess really did identify himself with prisoners, this tells us that a component of an individual's package of beliefs about oneself can remain entirely dormant, far removed from activation, while still persisting as an entity within that package. As we shall see later, Hoess occasionally and very selectively activated his 'prisoner identification' to serve as a convenient crutch to his self-esteem.

20. I have some personal, although indirect, knowledge of Dachau. Two Jewish men from my village were sent to Dachau after one of the round-ups in the mid-1930s. One of them was our neighbor. When the

men returned home, after about six months, I could not recognize our neighbor. Six years later, when the next round-up came and he faced the likelihood of going back to a concentration camp, he committed suicide.

21. Hoess, *Commandant of Auschwitz*, p. 85.

22. Franz Stangl, the commandant of the Sobibor and Treblinka concentration camps, made the identical claim. This is described in Gitta Sereny's book, *Into That Darkness* (New York: McGraw-Hill, 1974). Sereny examined Stangl's participation in evil in great depth, using extensive interviews with him, his wife, and associates. She found in him a man who, earnestly and sincerely, it seems, retained real misgivings about the Nazi ideology and its program of murders, but who performed murders so enthusiastically that he received an official commendation for being the most efficient concentration camp chieftain in Poland. He was a man who got pleasure from meeting the challenges confronting him in his daily murderous work. Stangl became involved in concentration camp administration incrementally, beginning with the mass killing of mentally or physically handicapped children.

23. Hoess, *Commandant of Auschwitz*, p. 88.

24. Ibid.

25. Ibid.

26. For a superb portrayal of the English butler, demonstrating honor through self-created dignity, see Kazuo Ishiguro, *The Remains of the Day* (New York: Vintage, 1989).

27. Pierre Boulle, *The Bridge on the River Kwai*, trans. X. Fielding (London: Vanguard Press, 1961).

28. Hoess, *Commandant of Auschwitz,* p. 170–171.

29. Ibid., p. 141.

30. A similar pattern—of supporting a package even though they had serious doubts about some of its component parts—occurs among American hospital surgeons. In their dealings with patients, they present a package of ideas that, together, amount to a claim of medical *certainty*. That package is made up of ideas such as "Surgeons definitely know what they are doing"; "they intervene to solve problems"; "they are confident that the outcome of their intervention will be positive." When these same surgeons talk with pathologists they often adhere to an entirely different package of ideas, including considerable doubt and uncertainty about their surgical efforts. While talking with pathologists, surgeons sometimes express annoyance at patients for placing them in

no-win situations, where failure is inevitable. Fred E. Katz, *Autonomy and Organization*, Part II.

31. In her Introduction to Bernd Naumann, *Auschwitz: A Report on the Proceedings Against Robert Karl, Ludwig Mulka and Others Before the Court at Frankfurt*, trans. J. Steinberg (New York: Praeger, 1966).

32. Ibid. pp. xxvi–xxvii.

33. Hoess was not included in this trial because he had been tried and executed eighteen years earlier. The main source is B. Naumann, *Auschwitz*. The following report deals only with culture of cruelty at the Auschwitz camp. But there is every indication that comparable phenomena existed at other concentration camps. Yitzhak Arad, writing about the Belzec, Sobibor, and Treblinka camps, says: "[SS men] constantly displayed initiative in trying to improve the extermination process. An integral aspect of their duties was that they were also to exhibit cruelty toward their victims, and many of them contributed their own 'ideas' and innovations," leading to reputations for specialized cruelty. Yitzhak Arad, *Belzec, Sobibor, Treblinka: The Operation of Reinhard Death Camps* (Bloomington: Indiana University Press, 1987), p. 198.

34. Naumann, *Auschwitz*, p. 103.

35. Ibid., p. 4.

36. Ibid., p. 205.

37. Ibid., p. 156.

38. Ibid., p. 115.

39. Ibid., p. 137.

40. Ibid., p. 123.

41. Ibid., p. 113.

42. Ibid., p. 282.

43. Ibid., p. 306.

44. Ibid., p. 308.

45. Ibid., p. 117.

46. Ibid., p. 202.

47. Ibid., p. xxxix.

48. Cited in ibid., p. xxix.

49. Ibid., p. xxvii.

50. Ibid., p. xxix.

51. Ibid., p. xiv.

52. Ibid., p. 267.

53. Ibid., p. 245.

54. Ibid., p. 133.

55. These are the words of Robert J. Lifton, in *The Nazi Doctors,* p. 351.

56. Introduction to Naumann, *Auschwitz,* p. xxviii.

57. Ibid., p. 93.

58. This is reported in John Bierman's *Righteous Gentile: The Story of Raoul Wallenberg, Missing Hero of the Holocaust* (New York: Viking Press, 1981).

59. See Melvin Kohn, *Class and Conformity: A Study in Values,* 2d ed. (Chicago: University of Chicago Press, 1977). Kelman and Hamilton, *Crimes of Obedience.*

60. In John Sack, *Lieutenant Calley: His Own Story* (New York: Viking Press, 1971).

61. Ibid., p. 126.

62. Seymour Hersh, *My Lai 4: A Report on the Massacre and Its Aftermath* (New York: Random House, 1970), p. 20.

63. Ibid., p. 43.

64. Sack, *Lieutenant Calley,* p. 85.

65. Hersh, *My Lai,* p. 47.

66. These figures were purely fictitious. They were intended for publicity and for reporting to higher army officials. They illustrate the manufacture of body count statistics.

67. Hersh, *My Lai,* pp. 54–56.

68. Ibid., p. 56.

CHAPTER 4. CONCLUSION: TURNING AWAY FROM EVIL

1. Recall, I have been defining evil as behavior ranging from depriving a person of dignity to depriving a person of life. Depriving a person of dignity is a critical starting point in the genesis of evil.

2. This technology was relatively new in the 1950s, when my research was done. Now, of course, it is not new any more. This and some other laboratory technology has changed in the intervening time.

3. President Lincoln's insistence, up to the summer of 1862, that the Civil War was being fought over the issue of preserving the Union rather than slavery, may have reinforced Lee's priorities when he made his initial decision to join the Confederacy and to reject President Lincoln's offer to command the Union forces. When Lincoln finally issued the Emancipation Proclamation, declaring the freeing of slaves to be a major objective of the Civil War, it introduced a new rider—a new dominant item that transformed the Union's package of objectives. As a consequence the war's priorities were suddenly and drastically rearranged, resulting in a new sense of vitality for the Union cause. To be sure the new focus led to considerable opposition to Lincoln among some Northerners. But in the eyes of many the new rider transformed the war into a moral crusade—for human freedom—that transcended the political objective of keeping the country united.

4. I am convinced that these ideas barely scratch the surface. There surely are many more ways in which the component parts within packages are structured.

5. Ted Robert Gurr, writing in the *Newsletter of the Center for International Development and Conflict Management*, University of Maryland (Fall 1989).

6. In a chapter titled "Nuremberg: The Failure of Law" Peter Haas writes: "[At the trials] Nazi leaders were treated as criminals, not as people conscientiously conducting themselves according to a new and widely held notion of right and wrong." *Morality after Auschwitz: The Radical Change of the Nazi Ethic* (Philadelphia: Fortress Press, 1988) p. 214.

7. I believe that war crimes trials serve the useful purpose of holding people accountable for their actions. But I also believe that we have vastly exaggerated expectations of what such trials can accomplish.

8. There is also the matter of how high (or low) is the threshold to the activation of a new rider and its attendant new behaviors. The current American family's readiness to divorce is a case of a low threshold to the activation of new riders. Here new riders—such as one announcing this marriage no longer works—are easily activated, thus fracturing the existing marriage because dormant resentments among the partners are activated when given legitimacy by the new rider.

9. This is a theme of Zygmunt Bauman's *Modernity and the Holocaust.*

10. George M. Kren and Leon Rappoport, *The Holocaust and the Crisis of Human Behavior* (New York: Holmes and Meier Publications, 1980), p. 133.

11. To give just one non-Western example, "The Rape of Nanking" by Japanese soldiers, upon entering the undefended city of Nanking on December 13, 1937. There, thousands upon thousands of innocent, unarmed people were raped and murdered. See Jonathan D. Spence, *The Search for Modern China* (New York: W. W. Norton, 1990).

For another example of a Holocaust culture of cruelty, see Christopher R. Browning, *Ordinary Men: Reserve Police Battalion 101 and the Final Solution in Poland* (New York: Harper Collins, 1992). Browning's book shows, just as this book shows, that ordinary people can commit the crassest horrors with real zeal, despite very little ideological commitment to evil; and, in the words of Walter Reich, a noted psychiatrist who reviewed the Browning book for the *New York Times* (April 12, 1992) it shows the powerful effect of the immediate situation in which people find themselves, situations in which it seems to the participants in the ghastliest of activities that they are not violating their moral codes.

This book operates from the conviction that it is precisely from within immediate situations in which people find themselves—be they outrageous and unusual or entirely mundane and ordinary—that we can discover ingredients that can enable us to exercise control over some of the social horrors we inflict on one another. And furthermore, that recognizing the ordinariness of evildoing does not mean that we should give up in despair. Quite the contrary. It means that we should get on with the task of finding out just what are the ingredients of that ordinariness in human behavior that are so conducive to evildoing. I hope this book shows that we can actually do this.

REFERENCES

Adorno, T., E. Frenkel-Brunswik, D. J. Levinson, and R. N. Sanford. *The Authoritarian Personality*. New York: Harper and Row, 1950.

Arad, Y. *Belzec, Sobibor, Treblinka: The Operation Reinhard Death Camps*. Bloomington: Indiana University Press, 1987.

Arendt, H. *Eichmann in Jerusalem: A Report on the Banality of Evil*. New York: Penguin Books, 1964.

Askenasy, H. *Are we all Nazis?* Secaucus, N.J.: Lyle Stuart, 1978.

Bauman, Z. *Modernity and the Holocaust*. Ithaca, N.Y.: Cornell University Press, 1989.

Bezwinska, J., and D. Czech, eds. *KL Auschwitz Seen by the SS: Hoess, Broad, Kremer*, 2d ed. Oswiecimiu: Publications of the Panstwowe Muzeum, 1978.

Bierman, J. *Righteous Gentile: The Story of Raoul Wallenberg, Missing Hero of the Holocaust*. New York: Viking Press, 1981.

Boulle, P. *The Bridge on the River Kwai*, trans. X. Fielding. London: Vanguard Press, 1961.

Browning, C. R. *Ordinary Men: Reserve Battalion 101 and the Final Solution in Poland*. New York: Harper Collins, 1992.

Cavendish, R. *The Power of Evil in Western Religion, Magic and Folk Belief*. New York: Putnam, 1975.

Conquest, R. *Harvest of Sorrow: Collectivization and the Terror of Famine*. New York: Oxford University Press, 1986.

Dostoevski, F. *The Brothers Karamazov*. New York: New American Library, Signet Edition, 1960.

Eliot, G. *Twentieth Century Book of the Dead*. New York: Charles Scribner's Sons, 1972.

Fackenheim, E. *God's Presence in History*. New York: New York University Press, 1970.

Fein, H. *Accounting for Genocide: National Responses and Jewish Victimization During the Holocaust*. Chicago: University of Chicago Press, 1979.

Gurr, T. R. *Newsletter of the Center for International Development and Conflict Management,* University of Maryland (Fall 1989).

Haas, P. J. *Morality After Auschwitz: The Radical Challenge of the Nazi Ethic.* Philadelphia: Fortress Press, 1988.

Hammer, R. *The Court-Martial of Lt. Calley.* New York: Coward, McGann, Geoghegan, 1971.

Hersh, S. *My Lai 4: A Report on the Massacre and Its Aftermath.* New York: Random House, 1970.

Hoess, R. *Commandant of Auschwitz,* trans. C. Fitz-Gibbon. New York: World Publishing Company, 1959.

Horowitz, I. L. *Taking Lives: Genocide and State Power.* New Brunswick, N.J.: Transaction Books, 1980.

Ishiguro, K. *The Remains of the Day.* New York: Vintage Books, 1989.

Katz, F. E. *Autonomy and Organization: The Limits of Social Control.* New York: Random House, 1968.

———. "Implementation of the Holocaust: The Behavior of Nazi Officials." *Comparative Studies in Society and History* (July 1982).

———. "A Sociological Perspective to the Holocaust." *Modern Judaism* (October 1982).

Kelman, H. C., and V. L. Hamilton. *Crimes of Obediences: Toward a Social Psychology of Authority and Responsibility.* New Haven, Conn.: Yale University Press, 1989.

Koestler, A. *Janus.* New York: Vintage Books, 1979.

Kohn, M. *Class and Conformity: A Study in Values,* 2d ed. Chicago: University of Chicago Press, 1977.

Kren, G. M., and L. Rappoport. *The Holocaust and the Crisis of Human Behavior.* New York: Holmes and Meier Publications, 1980.

Levi, P. *Survival in Auschwitz and the Reawakening.* New York: Summit Books, 1986.

Lifton, R. J. "The Medicalization of Killing." *Psychiatry* (Fall 1982).

———. *The Nazi Doctors: Medical Killing and the Psychology of Genocide.* New York: Basic Books, 1986.

Milgram, S. *Obedience to Authority: An Experimental View.* New York: Harper and Row, 1974.

Naumann, B. *Auschwitz: A Report on the Proceedings Against Robert Karl, Ludwig Mulka and Others Before the Court at Frankfurt,* trans. J. Steinberg. New York: Praeger, 1966.

Newman, J. *The World of Mathematics*, vol. I. New York: Simon and Schuster, 1956.

Rubenstein, R. *After Auschwitz*. Indianapolis: Bobbs-Merrill, 1975.

Sack, J. *Lieutenant Calley: His Own Story*. New York: Viking Press, 1971.

Seeskin, K. "The Reality of Radical Evil," *Judaism* (Fall 1980).

Segev, T. *Soldiers of Evil: The Commandants of the Nazi Concentration Camps*. New York: McGraw-Hill, 1987.

Sereny, G. *Into that Darkness*. New York: McGraw-Hill, 1974.

Spence, J. D. *The Search for Modern China*. New York: W. W. Norton, 1990.

Solzhenitsyn, A. *The Gulag Archipelago*, vol. 1. New York: Harper and Row, 1973.

Warner, S. A. *I Passed This Way*. New York: Alfred A. Knopf, 1979.

INDEX

153